GOING NINJA

GOING NINJA

THE 8 NEW RULES
FOR TODAY'S SILENT ASSASSINS

Samuel Kaplan and Keith Riegert

Ulysses Press

Published by:
Ulysses Press
P.O. Box 3440
Berkeley, CA 94703
www.ulyssespress.com

ISBN: 978-1-56975-861-8
Library of Congress Control Number: 2010937121

Printed in Canada by Webcom

10 9 8 7 6 5 4 3 2 1

Acquisitions Editor: Keith Riegert
Managing Editor: Claire Chun
Editor: Richard Harris
Proofreader: Lauren Harrison
Interior design and layout: what!design @ whatweb.com
Interior illustrations: see page 216
Cover design: Keith Riegert
Front cover photos: ninja © Keith Riegert; tiger © kerdog818/
    istockphoto.com; background © Mario7/shutterstock.com
Back cover photo: © Keith Riegert

Distributed by Publishers Group West

For Pickles

TABLE OF CONTENTS

HOW THE AUTHORS *WENT NINJA*

Dear Reader,

A couple of months ago, your humble authors, Sam the Sinewy and Glorious Manparts Keith, became the first Americans of European lineage to successfully found an officially recognized ninja *ryu*—The Crappy Pants Ninja Venture of Oakland, California.

After a christening ceremony at a local Benihana, the two men sat together under the hazy glow of a fiery stove and, their spirits warmed by heated mugs of green-tea-infused sake, spoke of their good fortunes. Here they were, two seemingly normal Americans, embraced by the world's deadliest art—*ninjutsu*. Theirs is a story that has *ended* beautifully. But the road to get there was rocky.

CRAPPY PRE-NINJA LIVES

Before becoming members of the world's most selective profession, your authors were normal American Joes. Much like you, dear reader, they were overweight, underemployed and unhappy. The unremarkable citizens went by the nonthreatening names of Sam Daisy Kaplan and Keith Sunshine Riegert. They spent their days bloated and depressed, not knowing the tremendous feeling of wielding a sharpened sword.

Lacking motivation and self-discipline, Sam had resigned himself to working as a paralegal for his mother. Keith's life, similarly miserable, consisted of a monotonous nine-to-five at the local Go-Go Happy Cupcake.

Why did they allow themselves to live enshrouded in the darkened mists of banality? The answer is comfort. Like most Americans, these pitiful specimens were content to be, well, content. They had tricked themselves into stagnation through a series of compromises. Their mediocre jobs may have sucked, but at least they came home to decent apartments, replete with both cable television *and* Internet. They had opted for security over happiness and safety over any sense of adventure.

Little did they know, however, that that deep-rooted sense of security was nothing more than a hellish façade. They would never be safe. No one ever is.

As you Americans live your quiet little lives, your world slowly fills with a vengeful new threat you've never heard about. Sure, your TVs constantly flicker with new media-born threats—terrorism, swine flu, economic collapse, killer flamingos, geriatric obesity—but no one ever bothers to discuss the serious and deadly threat that lurks in the shadows of our neighborhoods, homes and offices—the ninja.

It would be convenient to blame your collective ignorance on the stealthiness of the American ninjas themselves; but the truth is that you have no one to blame but yourselves. The signs are there: a movement in the shadows of a dark alleyway; a rustling in the trees despite a marked lack of wind; a man dressed as a ninja clinging to the ledge of an apartment building. You just choose to ignore them.

ATTACKED BY NINJAS

You see, though they didn't know it at the time, Keith and Sam shared a vindictive mutual friend—Michael P. Waterman. An old high school acquaintance, Michael had an intense jealousy for both Keith's job at Go-Go Happy Cupcake and Sam's flighty girlfriend, Nicki Johnson.

Typical of his passive-aggressive approach to life, Michael chose to hire ninjas to kill Keith and Sam instead of expressing his conflicted desires outright. Short on funds, Michael chose the cheap and efficient Majestic Foot Ninja Clan, an inexperienced ninja group whose members had previously been part of a traveling tap-dance troupe. Needless to say, while they had good footwork, their weapon's skills left something to be desired, and they lacked the necessary discipline to be deadly ninja warriors.

HOW OBESITY SAVED THE DAY

On a moonless Monday night, Sam and Keith walked through the parking lot of an In-N-Out Burger, clutching greasy Double-Doubles and fountain sodas. It was here, among the cars, trucks and oil stains that the ninjas sprang their violent trap. The ensuing battle was horrendous. The six ninjas that initiated the attack fought viciously, jumping from car roofs, slashing tires and rocketing ninja stars into dashboards and bumpers. Sam and Keith, in turn, fought for their lives. They flailed, kicked and cried, haphazardly throwing meat patties, syrupy shakes and delicious French fries.

NINJAS IN AMERICA?

Despite surviving relatively unscathed, Keith and Sam were severely rattled. America, they now knew, was no longer the safe haven it had once seemed. There was a new constant threat to cower from, a threat as serious as carpal tunnel, gingivitis and tainted eggs.

Like most uninformed Americans, the two of them had believed that the ancient practice of *ninjutsu* was an art that had long ago died in the fields of Japan, not one that was alive and well. Intrigued and terrified, they studied the practice from back to front, amassing a tremendous knowledge of the country's lurking threat. The ninja had to be dealt with, and they would have to be the dealers.

WHEN NINJAS ATTACK, THE WORLD'S MOST COMPREHENSIVE SURVIVAL GUIDE

Reluctantly, and fearing violent reprisal from the ninja community, Sam, Keith and a martial-arts master named Phoebe put their encyclopedic knowledge of the ninja into one incredibly important tome on survival, *When Ninjas Attack.*

They set out to answer the questions that could save people's lives: What is *ninjutsu*? How do ninjas train? What combat styles and weapons do they utilize? And what is the best way to defend yourself from a ninja attack?

For months, the budding ninja historians immersed themselves in the dark world of the icy-veined warriors. The tales they encountered were savage, nauseating and strangely beautiful. The deeper into the story of the ninja they went, the more respect they held for the art. They were falling in love with the ninja.

NINJA, A LOVE STORY

Sam and Keith soon discovered that being a ninja does not just mean a simple career as a deadly assassin. *Ninjutsu* is a full way of life. It is a diet, exercise routine, philosophy and creative outlet all wrapped up into one neat package. They discovered that ninjas enjoy miraculously little stress and lofty confidence levels; these warriors can live to unfathomable old ages and often engage in inspiring amounts of sex. The life of the ninja is, in a word, perfect.

Even as their anti-ninja survival guide was hitting store shelves, Sam and Keith were beginning to convert. They were going ninja.

THE PATH TO BECOME A NINJA: MORE DIFFICULT THAN IT APPEARS

Despite their full-fledged desires to become masters of the dark art, Keith and Sam almost immediately ran into one huge obstacle: They didn't know any real ninjas. The only ninjas they had met at that point were the poseurs who had attacked them.

An online search, including a dozen Craigslist "man-4-ninja" personal ads, turned up nothing but a handful of frightening encounters with sexually aggressive warrior wannabes.

Discouraged, Sam and Keith decided to go it alone, reading up on ninja moves and improving their strength, dexterity and flexibility at a karate-Pilates combo class at their local community center.

ENTER ME, DAZZLE SWORD DONALD,
REAL NINJA

Finally, after months of self-taught *ninjutsu* and intense stretching, Sam and Keith had reached a wall. I, Dazzle Sword Donald, real ninja, had been watching them from afar. They were as devoted to the ninja cause as anyone I'd ever seen, but needed the guidance of a real ninja. After a mediocre Pilates lesson, I approached them and invited them to tea. Over the course of several hours, we would seal the bonds of a friendship that would change the lives of Sam and Keith forever.

I knew these two budding amateur ninjas were eager for some formal ninja training, but they were hesitant in taking me on as a sensei. At the time, I was dressed in my everyday disguise (tie-dyed Grateful Dead T-shirt, red balloon pants and worn leather Birkenstocks), and I don't think they thought of me as a real ninja. They probably thought, "Is this guy for real?" Picking up on their skepticism, I threw down a ridiculously impressive cartwheel, injuring a number of passersby.

"But what's with the getup?" they asked. Over the course of drinking a half-dozen pots of oolong green tea at a Starbucks, I explained the ins and outs of the American ninja. In America, I told them, ninjas have evolved beyond the traditions of ancient Japan. American ninjas can no longer walk around in traditional black ninja outfits; instead, we need to blend in with our American surroundings lest we run the risk of the worst types of ostracism. My cover, I explained, was the traveling hippy.

Throughout the eye-opening Starbucks experience, I displayed several incredible handstands, an awe-inspiring somersault and several more equally impressive cartwheels. After the conversation, I walked up to the barista and froze her with a carefully crafted gaze of seduction. She promptly tore off her work apron and threw her arms around my hemp poncho. That, I think, really hooked them. Going ninja was their destiny.

THEY TRAIN; THEY BLEED;
THEY BECOME NINJA

The transition to ninja was not as easy as they thought it would be. They began with a humiliating karate class. Sweaty, bloody and bruised, the two twentysomethings went up against battle-hardened 11 and 12 year olds.

After healing, they turned their focus to the ninja basics: running, strength training, armed combat and aerial acrobatics. For hours, the ninjas-in-training meditated on sacks of old barley. Miraculously, a month later, they had transformed themselves into six-pack-flexing ninjas, imbued with the self-discipline only possessed by ninjas and a few very focused mimes. Just six weeks after deciding to become ninjas, they had done it. They had gone ninja. It was time for them to join a clan.

Tryouts for a ninja clan tend to be violent, to say the least. One of your authors lost two fingers and his left big toe. The other forfeited several gallons of blood and a small portion of his kidney. They were beaten, stabbed, punched and kicked. They were graded harshly on cartwheel technique and execution. Out of 41 ninja novices attempting to join the clans, 37 had died. The honor of survival was breathtaking.

THE AWESOME LIFE OF THE NINJA

Needless to say, since that day, the lives of your authors have been more incredible than they could have ever imagined. According to their tax returns, each earned nearly $10,000 over the last year. They have had several girls express interest in potential dates.

THEY DECIDE TO SPREAD THE LOVE

Anyway, a few months ago, Keith and Sam decided they should sit down and write about their experiences. The people of America needed to know about the journey to becoming a ninja.

So, without further ado, here it is, in all its glory, a detailed account of what you can expect along the path. But be warned: You will bleed. You will vomit. You will cry. There is a 64-percent chance that you will die. So think long and think hard: Do you have what it takes to *go ninja?*

> — Dazzle Sword Donald
> 7th Degree Ninja
> Brotherhood of the Shadow Ryu, CLAN Dragon

NINJAS AND AMERICA: A HISTORY SOAKED IN FRIENDSHIP, PHILOSOPHY AND BLOOD

"America should not fear the ninja; it should hold the ninja's hand, brew him a pot of green oolong tea, fix him a sandwich and thank him for centuries of hard work."

— President John F. Kennedy

Ninja. There, to the left of this sentence, sits the most terrifying word in America. Many terms have tried to unseat *ninja* as America's most terrifying—communism, terrorism, swine flu, tainted broccoli—but none has come close. Chances are, judging from the frightening subject matter of this paragraph, that you've already peed yourself a little. You're debating whether you should read on. Maybe you should just put the book down and go get yourself a frozen yogurt with sprinkles. You, like almost all Americans, imagine the *shinobi* warrior as a dire threat to your peaceful existence. But ask yourself, is your fear warranted? Is the ninja really the enemy you think he is? Do you actually understand anything about the ninja? Probably not.

You see, in contrast to common perception, ninjas have been friends to Americans since Benjamin Franklin was wearing diapers. In a certain sense, they are the very foundation upon which this great empire was built.

✳ ✳ ✳
NINJAS IN COLONIAL AMERICA

Did you know? Five quick facts about the Ninja in early America

- The United States of America is named after Hideki Americamoto, the first ninja to reach North America.
- The word *black* was coined by ninja clothing designer Georgio Hikasaki in 1722.
- The idiom "one [bird] in the hand is worth two in the bush" was adapted from the ninja saying "one [star] in the head is worth two in the leg."
- The state of Connecticut was named after the ninja weapon and stationery store Connect & Cut, the first superstore in the 13 colonies.
- The American flag went through many incarnations before becoming the version we know today. Controversy erupted early on when the traditional lethal ninja stars were replaced by lame five-pointed versions.

The original Stars and Stripes

Here's a scary fact: In its early years, America was a bustling ninja haven. Pushed out of Japan in the 1600s, ninjas found a welcoming new home in the loose and lawless colonies of the New World. While a few settled in small towns or established simple farming communities, most were attracted to the bright lamplight of early America's growing urban centers. City neighborhoods like Ninjatown in New York City (now "SoHo") and Shuriken's Landing in Philadelphia sprang up like bamboo stalks in a freshly mulched enemy corpse.

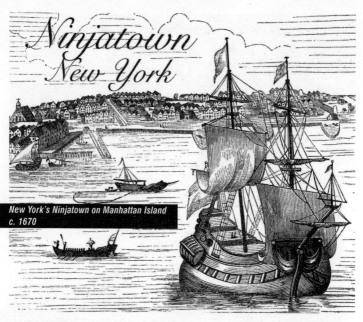

New York's Ninjatown on Manhattan Island c. 1670

The influence of these colonial ninjas on the young country was profound. Early on, when colonists were having trouble gaining the trust of the natives, ninjas helped bridge the gap by providing helpful bartering suggestions and language lessons in both Apache and Blackfoot.

Later, when the settlers began to build townships and cities, ninjas helped pound in the nails of the homes and buildings that created America. While they did assassinate several unfortunate European colonists, they also helped to establish North America's earliest schools, businesses, farmlands and sword emporiums.

NINJAS AND THE BRITISH

As tensions rose between the colonists and the Brits, ninjas sided with the settlers on several landmark incidents.

The Boston Tea Party: Frustrated by unfair tax laws, several colonists decided to stage a protest and ruin a shipment of tea. Ninjas, equally upset that the British Tea Company was shipping black tea instead of green, joined the colonists as they tossed the boat load of tea bags into the sea.

Creation of American Accents: Looking to find a way to distinguish themselves from British landowners, colonists turned to local ninja clans to help them create a less pretentious patois, today's thick New York accent.

Training of Soldiers: With tensions reaching an all time high, Americans began training soldiers for the looming war. Knowing that Americans lacked sufficient military expertise, George Washington hired ninjas to train the fledgling Continental Army. The experience led Washington to proclaim, "Firearms are second only to the ninja in importance; they are the people's liberty's teeth."

NINJAS AND AMERICA'S CONSTITUTION

Immediately following the War of Independence, it came time to for the Founding Fathers to establish an ideological foundation for their new country. Lacking experience, they turned to the well-organized ninja clans for guidance.

When James Madison first sat down to draft the amendments to the Constitution, he turned to the most esteemed set of laws he knew—the *Koga Green Tea Brewing Company Employee Manual*.

THE KOGA GREEN TEA BREWING COMPANY EMPLOYEE MANUAL

Laws

Accord I

Freedoms, Petitions, Assembly

The Big Tea Boss shall make no law respecting an establishment of religion, or prohibiting the free exercise thereof; or abridging the freedom of speech, or of the gossip mongers, or the right of the employees peaceably to assemble, and to petition the Management for a redress of grievances.

Accord II

Right to Bear Swords and Other Vital Weaponry

A well-regulated ninja battalion, being necessary to the security of a well-run and successful Tea Brewing Company, the right of the employees to keep and bear Swords and Other Vital Weaponry, shall not be infringed.

THE DECLARATION OF INDEPENDENCE

The Constitution wasn't the only document the Founding Fathers lifted from classic ninja doctrine. And when Thomas Jefferson penned his initial draft of the Declaration of Independence, he touched quill to paper and proclaimed, "Equal rights for all, special privileges for ninjas!"

DRAFT PREAMBLE TO THE DECLARATION OF INDEPENDENCE, 1776

We hold this truth to be self-evident, that all Ninjas are created equal, that they are endowed by the Dark Art with certain unalienable and bloody Rights, that among these are Life, Liberty and the Pursuit of Cold Revenge. That to secure these rights, Ninjas are trained among the Greatest of Men, deriving their just powers from the deep Roots of Skill and Honor, That whenever any Form of Government becomes destructive of these ends, it is the Right of the Ninja to throw down Sick Moves, and to institute new Order. . .

Though the final draft of the Declaration would not include the words *ninja*, *ninjas* or even *disemboweled intestines*, it was nevertheless a glorious time for the *shinobi* in America. So what happened? How could the ninja's seemingly indelible status in American history have been completely washed over and erased?

A NINJA DIVIDED
AGAINST ITSELF CANNOT STAND

After the War for Independence, the ninja's lofty status gradually declined. Lengthy breaks between wars meant few soldiers to train, and American politicians had little reason to curry favor with the secretive warriors. No longer needed by the government, Americans began to see their ninja neighbors as potentially violent threats. A large faction of the populace wanted the ninjas gone.

By the 1850s, as a result of this anti-ninja sentiment, America's ninja population split violently in two. The first group known as the Western Shinobi, a faction of unruly, ruthless ninjas, was bent on spreading the ninja gospel from sea to shining sea. They were opposed vehemently by the second group, the Eastern Ninjas, who feared that such Western expansion would result in violent reprisal from the U.S. government.

The result of this ideological clash was a five-year ninja battle that decimated the country's ninja population. During the battle, over 4,000 non-ninjas were accidentally killed by stray throwing knives and poorly aimed arrows. By 1855, there were fewer than 1,000 ninjas in America, and Americans regarded these ninjas as an unwanted threat. The resulting backlash from the non-ninja population forced the remaining members underground. The names and accomplishments of America's first ninjas were lost forever.

Ten years after the start of the Great Ninja War, the ninja was but an artifact of America's early days. Those *shinobi* that had survived sought work in more traditionally acceptable professions—detective, soldier, sake brewer, stripper—and left the noble ninja life behind. The art of *ninjutsu* had fallen to shambles in the mighty U.S. of A. Those who continued on with the badass art did so in secret. How secret? By 1870, no one in America even knew the ninja existed.

THE NINJA RISES AGAIN

Something fascinating has happened in this country. The ninja, once popular during the birth of our great nation has, suddenly and miraculously, come back into favor. Similar to the epic hoopskirt, monocle and dumbwaiter fads of the 1990s, the ninja has made "1700s colonial" cool once again.

Yes, this is the age of the rising of the ninja, a glorious and fear-inducing time. And you should feel honored and terrified to be apart of it. However, the question still remains as to why the ninja is suddenly en vogue after being shunned for so long. Let's look at some of the factors:

1. The American empire is in the decline: Analysts agree that if there is one thing that can save this country, it is the ninja.

2. By 2020, 75 percent of Americans will be overweight. Intense, calorie-burning *ninjutsu* training may be the only way to significantly lower your risk of becoming obese.

3. Gasoline is becoming more expensive in the U.S., making traditional ninja transport, such as running, jumping, roller skating and tiger riding much more cost-efficient.

4. As America becomes more partisan, citizens are looking for new ways to protect themselves from either the liberals or conservatives.

5. Television has, once again, romanticized the *shinobi* warrior in TV shows such as *So You Want to Be a Ninja, Throwing at the Stars* and *Man vs. Ninja vs. Bear.*

Moreover, the ninja encompasses a part of American life that has been washed away in today's sad society—badassery. In a land now dominated by hybrid minivans, soy-based sausages and quiet yoga studios, the age-old art of killing has been all but lost. Think about it. How many of your friends could even kill an unarmed grizzly bear? Who among your family can successfully wield a *katana* or *ninja-to* in defense against a marauding mountain lion? Not many.

Thus, the resurgence of the ninja is almost predictable. As America becomes fatter, lazier and wussier, the counterbalance—the ninja— becomes stronger. Tomorrow we may well be a nation of silent assassins. That's why you're here, right? To join the future? To earn your *tenugui*? To become ninja?

Your heart is racing right now. You're having some doubts. Maybe you should just join a coed softball team. That's American, right? *Yabē!*

Wrong! There is nothing more American than being a ninja. Sack up.

You need to take the time to ask yourself some important questions:

1. Am I okay with a couple stab wounds?
2. When standing on the edge of a cliff, do I feel exhilaration or terror?
3. If required, could I do a front flip over a bucket of venomous pit vipers?
4. How would I rate my tiger-riding skills (both bareback and western)?
5. Do I look good in black?

If you answered these simple questions correctly, congratulations, you're about to embark on an intense, awe-inspiring life transformation!

Take some time to write a couple of goodbye letters. Make out a will (just in case). And get ready to *go ninja*.

NINJA GLOSSARY

VITAL NINJA TERMS FOUND IN THIS BOOK

The following terms will be found numerous times throughout this guide to becoming a ninja. While you may think you already know most of these terms, your understanding of them may be false.

Ninjasapien letalis

Ninja: 1. *noun:* Any person highly trained in the martial art of *ninjutsu*. A professional ninja is employed for services such as espionage and assassination. 2. *adjective:* Staggeringly amazing to the point of inducing awe-inspired death. *Usage:* "You finished that accounting projection already? Very ninja, Dale!"

Ninjutsu: "The ninja's art," *ninjutsu* is the school of training that prepares ninja students in swordplay, knife throwing, unarmed combat, stealth, disguise, espionage, explosives, artisan baking and fine pottery.

America: The greatest country on earth. America's 3.8 million square miles of unbridled power are home to the world's most confident, fattest ninja population.

Tiger: A large, brightly colored apex predator and one of the world's four so-called big cats. The tiger is often mistaken to be the legendary beast *ninjusa*, born when ninjas mate with American women.

Samurai: Classified as *Ninjasapien neanderthalis*, the samurai warriors of medieval Japan were the direct predecessors of the ninja. Steeped to a fault in tradition, samurai warriors dedicated their lives to one ruling shogun. Their backward sense of honor and less-than-stealthy tactics led to their eventual extinction at the hands of craftier ninja breeds.

Ninjasapien neanderthalis *(samurai)*

IMPORTANT NINJA ABBREVIATIONS

GNC (Global Ninja Coalition): The international governing body of ninjas, GNC "embassies" can be found in most major metropolitan areas. Often, local ninja clans hold meetings, bake sales and nutritional seminars at these busy locations.

ANC (American Ninja Convert): A subclass of the ninja, ANCs are American-born citizens who become ninjas after the age of two.

ANAL Exam (American Ninjutsu Aptitude Litmus Exam): Upon graduation, every ninja must take the painfully rigorous ANAL Exam. Three hours of multiple choice questions put your knowledge of five subjects to the ultimate test: ninja history, pressure points, combat strategy, weapon movements and intermediate algebra.

NINJA ACTIONS

Kick: The delivery of the foot to a target's face, body or groin. The weight and strength of the leg, combined with the length of reach, makes the kick one of the more powerful moves in the ninja arsenal.

Punch: (1) A thrusting blow delivered with the clenched hand or hands, used to inflict pain, damage or death upon an opponent. (2) A delicious ninja beverage combining unfiltered sake, rose petals and fresh wasabi.

Throw: A versatile *ninjutsu* skill in which the ninja projects either (1) a sharpened object at a person or (2) a person at a sharpened object.

Front Roll: A swift defensive maneuver by which a ninja tucks his head into his crotch and rolls forward, thus evading an assault and protecting his lineage.

Cartwheel: A graceful sideways spin performed by a ninja in training, battle and ballet.

Death: The everlasting desistance of all vital functions in an organic being. According to Department of Health statistics, death is most often brought about by (1) old age, (2) disease or (3) ninja.

Seppuku: Ritualistic suicide performed by ninjas during rare moments of shame. To commit *seppuku*, the ninja takes his sword and casually inserts it into their rippling abdomen.

NINJA LIQUIDS

Sake: Considered the "Gatorade of the East," sake is a delicious, refreshing, nonfattening alcoholic beverage made from fermented rice and flavored with a pinch of virgin's blood. For the majority of ninjas, sake takes the place of water for hydrating the body. Remember the common saying: "When life gives you lemons, squeeze the aforementioned lemons into opponent's eyeballs. Then enjoy cool sake."

Blood: Blood is the bodily fluid that carries vital elements and nutrients to internal organs through a series of arteries and veins. Similar to the Western adage about milk, many ninja families remind their children, "There's no use crying over spilt blood."

THE NINJA SENSES

Sight: The ability to see shapes, colors and blood.

Hearing: The ability to audibly sense the swish of a rival ninja sword.

Touch: The ability to feel a target's final heartbeat.

Smell: The ability to inhale and detect the scent of a cowering sweat.

Taste: The ability to sense the subtle flavor of adrenaline.

Nociception: The ability to sense the pain of an imbedded *shuriken*.

Equilibrioception: The ability to remain balanced while standing on a small post.

Proprioception and kinesthesia: Control over joint motion and acceleration when chasing down a fleeing drug lord.

Sense of time: The ability not to show up late to a fight.

Thermoception: The ability to sense a cool breeze brought on by a flying arrow.

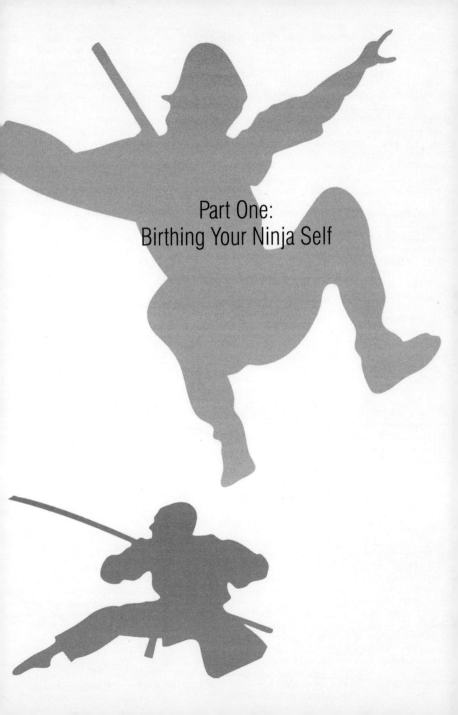

Part One:
Birthing Your Ninja Self

CHAPTER 1

THE 8 NEW RULES
OF THE
SILENT ASSASSIN

Until this point, you have passed your existence as a collection of unmotivated molecules waiting for some sort of magic catalyst to explode into your life. Well, guess what? The catalyst you have been waiting for has finally arrived, and you hold it in your delicate hands. Yes, this book, if you read it thoroughly and adhere to the training and diet suggestions outlined in its pages, is the key to your future. In 30 days, a change will take hold. You will be forever transformed from a sloppy, club-footed American no one into a quick-footed ninja someone.

This transformation will be grueling. You will face lethal states of physical exhaustion. The amount of crying you experience will leave you dehydrated. You will be forced to decide which of your favorite internal organs you would like to keep the most. You may die. But, should you make it through the next four weeks, you will emerge a stronger, sexier and deadlier person.

Once you've flipped, kicked and stabbed your way through your starting exercises and been accepted into the global ninja community, you must adopt the Eight New Rules for Today's Silent Assassin. The pinnacle of America-ninja synergy, this collection of simple maxims embodies the essence of today's modern American ninja. They are as ninja as a sharpened-steel *ninja-to* and as American as a freshly baked bald eagle pie.

A pair of GNC-approved, regulation 22-inch ninja-to.

The American classic bald eagle pie, delicious and nutritious.

✻ ✻ ✻

1. BE NINJA, BE AMERICAN

Even after you've accrued a six-pack and the mental iciness of a komodo dragon, you must never turn your back on the country from whose teat you were suckled. Lift that star-spangled banner above your head proudly, continue to watch *Dancing with the Stars* and never forget that being American means, above all, feeling vaguely superior to ninjas from other countries without knowing anything about them.

A ninja living the American Dream.

✻ ✻ ✻

2. BE MODERN

Don't let 1,000 years of powerful ninja tradition keep you from living in the 21st century. While you may be constrained by tradition during battle, you should embrace the modern world in all its neon glory. Packing a mean singing voice behind that darkened mask? Head out on the town for karaoke night. Booked a job in New York, but live in Seattle? Forget the traditional horse and snag a seat on Ninjair, the airline of choice for business-savvy ninjas.

Ninjair ("Fly the Deadly Skies") offers fast, comfortable travel across the globe and now features the state-of-the-art Ninjato Seat, with more leg room and convenient storage for your swords, stars and lattes.

✳ ✳ ✳

3. BE CONNECTED

Laptops, tablets and smartphones not only make good throwing projectiles, but in today's urban and socially crowded world, it pays to stay connected. While modern ninjas are still executing their missions in old-fashioned ways, most American ninjas now use Web 2.0 to drum up business and maintain a national network of ninja colleagues. As a bonus, once you've completed your training and graduated, we'll open the door to a brand new world of Internet possibilities, from ninja social networks and assassin dating sites to online job postings and the world's fastest ninja-news source.

✳ ✳ ✳

4. BE TRADITIONAL

"No firearms, computers, corn syrup or robots" is the motto of the Beartooth Mountain Vegan Ninja Clan. Over the past seven centuries, the world has migrated from small sleepy villages that spawned the ninja into the big bustling cities that have no time for him. Staying true to a handful of ninja traditions will bring meaning into your life and in turn make you a better warrior. Start slow by hosting a sushi-rolling party. Make your way to the park, choose a tree and spend a few hours in deep, silent meditation. Stick to your traditional ninja garb of full black outfit and matching mask, even during the balmy summer months. Plant and tend your own rice paddy. And learn the subtle differences between your genmaicha, oolong and angry dragon green teas.

As a ninja, you should be able to sleep and meditate anywhere. Make sure to bring a pillow wherever you go.

5. BE

Being a ninja is more than mastering a lethal set of martial arts and honing your reflexes. It is a mind-set and a revolution of the brain muscle. To succeed as a ninja, you will be required to *think* like a ninja at all times. You should begin by strategizing elaborate escape routes from different rooms you enter—like your bathroom, office or coffee shop—and then execute these tactics at random. If anyone witnesses your escape, knock them out and try again. Soon enough, you'll find yourself planning phantom assassinations for everyone you come across without even thinking about it!

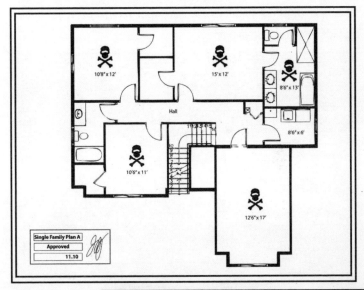

Every room you enter should be treated as a potential killing zone.

6. BE INDEPENDENTLY TRAINED

When it comes to wasting time and money, formal ninja finishing schools take the rice cake. These classic "institutions of higher belts" were the preferred avenue to hone prime skills and land a cushy "associate assassin" position right out of *ninjutsu* school. Today, however, Ninja universities are highly competitive and expensive, and carry no solid guarantee of job placement upon earning your ninth-degree black belt. With tuition and outside expenses setting you an average of $60,000 in the red, chances are you'll be starting your ninja career with a healthy amount of debt. The route of higher Ninjacation may have been a sure bet for the *shinobi* of your parents' generation, but it's a big gamble for you.

Ninja school is for rich ninjas and overachievers.

✳ ✳ ✳

7. BE AN UNTAMABLE CARTWHEELING MACHINE

You probably think the cartwheel is for sissies and schoolchildren. How little you understand, small grasshopper. The raw power of a well-executed cartwheel can blow an opponent away, and may very well get you laid, too. Known to ninjas as the *hoiru subarashii* (awesome wheel), the graceful, silent and quick cartwheel is both a terrifying weapon and a defensive escape move. For you, mastery of this ancient maneuver will be a challenge, but one that will eventually save your life.

A well-executed cartwheel can help you avoid an unpleasant obstacle like a landmine, puddle or dozing alligator.

8. BE YOURSELF

Remember, being a ninja does not necessarily mean reducing yourself to assassin or covert spy. In fact, it's best not to get fixated on the glamorous life of the professional killer or private dick, as they're two of the toughest and most competitive professions a ninja can pursue. Instead, think about your particular set of skills. Maybe you're good with pets. Why not become a tiger trainer? Or perhaps you have a discerning palate—why not become a personal *yakitori* chef? Whatever your skills, becoming a ninja will open professional doors you never knew existed.

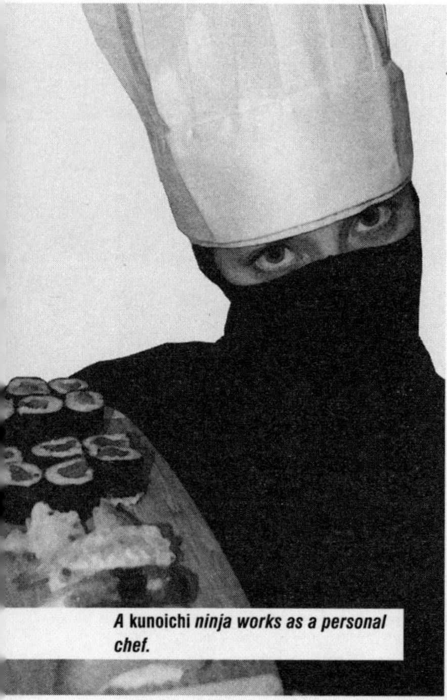

A* kunoichi *ninja works as a personal chef.

Popular Alternate Ninjafessions

- Aerobics Instructor
- Children's Gymnastics Coach
- Sword Tester
- Marketing Coordinator
- Tiger Trainer
- Sake Brew Master
- Personal Yakitori Chef

CHAPTER 2

ENTER THE NINJA: A BACKGROUND OF THE DARK ART

Many a regular Joe has blindly embarked upon the winding path to ninjahood only to find he doesn't know what the hell a ninja actually is. Do you? Before you become a twig on the tree of the ninja, you must first dig deep into the tree's roots and grasp the full history of the art.

This cave painting from the Koga region in Japan marks the first record of a ninja attack.

SIGNIFICANT MOMENTS IN NINJA HISTORY

200: Invention of the *Katana* (Japan's First Sword)

When a sushi chef is attacked by an ungrateful patron, he uses his largest sushi knife to stab his assailant. A well-known steel smelter named Hiro Tacuchimi witnesses the event while enjoying an Alaskan roll and, inspired by the sushi chef's innovative use of cutlery, gets the idea to manufacture knives designed specifically for the purposes of protection. Today, his *katana* and *ninja-to* are considered relics and sell to collectors for millions of dollars.

800–900: The Rise of the Samurai

Although many modern ninjas are reluctant to admit it, the path of the ninja was first paved by their primordial predecessors—the samurai. In the early ninth century, Emperor Kammu drafts an army to gain imperial control over all of Japan, but the soldiers he drums up are illiterate and lazy. Meanwhile, in Kyoto, a group of wealthy magistrates sense Kammu's vulnerability and conscripts a legion of warriors to defeat Kammu's army. These campaigns are successful, and the magistrates succeed in stealing Kammu's power, transforming Japan from an imperial monarchy into a collection of feudal regions. The magistrates reward the warriors for their services and loyalty by offering them lifelong employment, an unprecedented retirement package and significant tax breaks.

For the next 300 to 400 years, until the arrival of the ninja, the samurai dominates Japan's battlefields and hold the title of Japan's most badass warrior.

1307: Popping of the Ninja Cherry

Budding *shinobi* Mattari Sutorippu becomes the first ninja to record an official assassination. Before Sutorippu's famed

"Disembowelment Heard Round the World," early ninjas were frustratingly stalled at an assassin's "second base," repeatedly performing "hand jobs"—the act of brutally removing a victim's phalanges one by one.

1490: Accidental Discovery of the New World

On a hot morning in late summer, a ninja by the name of Hideki Americamoto accidentally discovers Malibu, California during a vigorous ocean swim from his Kuzakichō beach house.

1550: The First Giving of *Arigatō* (Invention of the California Roll)

After the discovery of the New World, ninjas make frequent jaunts across the ocean for afternoon picnics. In late fall of 1550, ninjas sit down for a formal meal with the Ohlone Indians, marking the first celebration of Giving of *Arigatō*. Having run out of real crab, the ninjas crafted an "imitation crab" out of pollock and quail eggs, marking the creation of the California roll.

1560–1650: Height of the Ninja

For nearly a century, ninjas enjoy overwhelming success as Japan's elite warriors and spies. With regional magistrates and lords constantly vying for more power and land, ninjas are in constant demand because of their excellent espionage and assassination skills. It is a prosperous epoch for the ninja, one remembered today as the First Peak of the Ninja. The Second Peak, modern ninjas predict, will come in the early 21st century.

1650–1980: The Ninja Underground

After the Battle of Kuso Forest, the ninja disappears from history. During what become known as the Dark Ages, ninjas participated in no battles, peacekeeping operations or festivals. As a result, the world falls into utter chaos.

So what happened to the ninja? Had he simply overstayed his welcome in the Empire of Japan? Not quite. Having dispatched a huge swath of the nobility, ninjas were forced to move on because they had assassinated nearly all of their potential clients. Out of work, they counted their earnings and set sail for a world untouched by the ninja's vicious sword.

During the 1700s, ninjas settled throughout the Western world. The migrant ninjas established underground colonies, training facilities and souvenir shops in cities from Athens, Greece, to Athens, Georgia.

1850–1900: A New and Noble Profession

During the 1800s, the term *ninja* is still synonymous with "braggart," "fandangler," "ballybrand-two-pence" and a number of other now-archaic insults. More importantly, ninja is a dangerous title to claim. To counteract the negative connotations of the profession, most ninjas choose a new and noble line of work—detective.

The Pinkerton National Detective Agency becomes the perfect cover profession for the resurgent ninja clans in the United States. Founded by a grandmaster ninja named Allan Satsu Pinkerton, the detective and spy agency quickly earns a reputation after first spoiling an assassination attempt on presidential candidate Abraham Lincoln and subsequently assisting in the assassination of President Lincoln just a few years later.

Besides employing the ninjas as urban detectives and bodyguards, the U.S. government also enlisted Pinkerton's agents to track the Wild West's most savage outlaws. Ninjas were responsible for the capture—and eventual hanging—of such infamous outlaws as Fancy Pants Brown, Hot Carl, Nice Thighs Malloy and, around the turn of the century, Famous Flatulence Foreman.

1914–Present: The Ninja Renaissance

It wasn't until 1914 that the true Ninja Renaissance began. During the Great War, ninjas from every walk of life join up to fight with the Allies and prove a fearsome force on the front lines. Afterward, as the Western world embraces everything Eastern, ninjas become a successfully integrated part of society. These "Western *shinobi*" adopt a delicate mix of old ninja custom and new Western style. They are a new breed of ninjas, accepted by the West and reviled by ninja traditionalists in the East.

2000: Hiro Matsumi and the "Let Them In" Speech

For generations, the ruling ninja body, the Sayōnara Ninja Coalition (SNC), had enforced a law prohibiting Western citizens from becoming officially sanctioned ninja practitioners. In his landmark speech *"Ni Sorera o Kika Sete* (Let Them In)," SNC President Hiro Matsumi, outlines his progressive plans to allow all ninjas into a new Global Coalition. The landmark transition is especially important for America's burgeoning ninja population. The Sayōnara Ninja Coalition is renamed the Global Ninja Coalition.

2010: Maine's Progressive Prop 459 (The Ninja Rights Initiative)

Maine becomes the first state in the union to formally acknowledge ninjas as citizens under a specially sanctioned ninja law. Ninjas in the Pine Tree State are allotted 13 assassinations per year without legal repercussion. The law also allows each ninja family to possess up to three full-grown tigers in an urban residence and up to twelve in rural areas.

CHAPTER 3

LEARNING ᴛʜᴇ FUNDAMENTALS ᴏꜰ NINJA DECEPTION

Why so still, kitty?
The lounging portly child asks
The hungry tiger

—anon. Japanese haiku A.D. 1325

✳ ✳ ✳

STEALTH

"Survival is an art; death, a hobby."

—Sharp Fingers Flanagan,
Irish Shinobi Brotherhood

To endure a day in the Northern Calcareous Alps, you must understand the elegance of the Austrian Waltz. To grasp the cutthroat strategy of Donald Trump, you must understand the delicate subtleties of the comb-over. And to live the life of a ninja, you must first understand the fundamental art of stealth.

Ninjutsu combat includes a complex arsenal of strikes, throws, grapples, evasive maneuvers and attacks with a variety of weapons. But behind every tool the ninja employs is an elementary focus on *stealth*. It is this incorporation of silence, concealment, disguise and distraction that lifts *ninjutsu* above every other form of combat and makes it the most deadly form of martial arts in the history of mankind.

To become a successful ninja, you must train your stealth abilities in as many different environments as possible: in the homestead, in city streets, on crowded beaches, through deciduous forests, over fields of barley, across babbling brooks, on horseback and underwater. By the end of your stealth training, you should feel as comfortable in drag in broad daylight as you would naked in a pitch-black room.

✳ ✳ ✳

SILENT MOVEMENT

One of the most important aspects of *ninjutsu* is *ohisa* (translated as "long time, no see")—the ability to move without making a sound. Americans are notoriously loud walkers (a fact you can most likely verify if you've ever lived in an apartment building), and learning to move silently is the first step to becoming a successful ninja and conscientious roommate.

Traditionally, training in silence began for ninjas at infancy, when baby students were muzzled to prevent any audible crying. At the age of

Shhhhhh.

eight, the septum was then ceremoniously removed to prevent somnolent snoring and daytime nasal wheezing. The young ninjas were taught to run across autumn leaves without making a single crunch, and they were taught to engage in ferocious battle without so much as rattling a blade of grass. To become full-fledged warriors, the young ninjas engaged in a silent 20-minute sword battle on a surface of bubble wrap.

Today, Silent Movement Training has morphed into more of a lifestyle pursuit than a series of difficult challenges:

1. Typing without audible key taps.

2. Eating cereal by crushing each piece with the tongue.

3. Speaking in an inside voice while on a cell phone.

4. Seducing a mate without uttering a single word.

5. Making love without your partner noticing.

✳ ✳ ✳

CONCEALMENT

In addition to traveling and fighting noiselessly, a well-trained ninja will use his environment to conceal him or herself from an opponent. While ninjas are adept at long distance *yumi* (bow and arrow) sniping, indoor and garden attacks require close-range combat skills. To gain the advantage of surprise, ninjas must be able to conceal themselves as inanimate objects and then execute a painful or lethal attack from an arm length's distance, causing the target to believe they have been viciously impaled by the office printer or ruthlessly slapped in the face by their favorite rosebush.

NIGHT MOVEMENT:
SEEING WITHOUT SEEING

Ninjas must be able to do more at night than just dance. In the time before electricity, ninjas enjoyed absolute nocturnal supremacy over their brightly dressed, ill-adapted foes. To obtain the night advantage, ninjas of both yesteryear and today spend months training blindfolded during the day and navigating the darkness of night in order to develop both keen night vision and the ability to "see" with the proximity senses of finger, nose and tongue.

Surveillance footage of an epic night-time ninja battle.

✳ ✳ ✳

HIDING

The ninja warrior is the most adept hide-and-seeker in the world. In old Japan, child ninjas would often begin a juvenile game of hide and seek, only to be finally discovered fully grown 20 years later.

For the adult ninja, the skill was utilized for espionage missions, assassinations and surprise birthday parties alike. On assassination missions, for example, ninjas would employ a host of hiding locales—stuffed into a target's mattress, straddling an entryway or curled beneath a huge pile of pillows.

THE INCREDIBLE STORY OF HIROO ONODA

When 2nd Lt. (and possible seventh-degree ninja) Hiroo Onoda made landfall on Lubang Island in the Philippines during World War II in 1945, he made a pledge to both his ninja clan and the Emperor of Japan that under no circumstances would he surrender his post. Utilizing his superior hiding skills, Lt. Onoda concealed himself so well that when the war finally ended eight months later, no one could find him to deliver the news. Forgotten by his superiors, Lt. Onoda continued to protect his hidden post diligently until 1974, when he was finally convinced to surrender.

Ninjas can hide anywhere.

With incredible dexterity, climbing skills and creativity, the well-trained ninja should be able to turn the most desolate landscape into one replete with hiding spots.

Once you have mastered simple hiding places (tree branches, telephone poles, sewer lines and closets), you must practice various forms of intricate concealment: carefully sewn in the back of your target's car seat, straddling the arch of a doorway for an afternoon or stuffed into a suitcase like a delicate blouse.

SURPRISE DEATHDAY PARTY

Surprisingly, the modern concept of the "surprise birthday party"
has its origins in the ninja tradition of the "surprise deathday
party." Ever the playful tricksters, ninjas would surprise their
victims with lavish parties followed by hails of sharpened gifts.

The following hiding places are listed from easiest to hardest. Try each
of them until you feel comfortable.

Tree branches: These lofty lookout points are easy to ascend, and
their chlorophyll canopies offer excellent concealment.

Dangling from a large chandelier: The distribution of your weight
will prove challenging, but a well-executed chandelier-dangle will give
you the leverage needed for a hard-to-counter surprise aerial attack.

Stuffed into a fully-loaded dishwasher while it's running:
Appliances in general make excellent places to lay in wait for an
unsuspecting enemy. The trick is to remain spry and dry despite your
cramped position and boiling hot conditions.

Frozen lakes: Although these hiding locales are only used for
assignments against ice-fisherman and Arctic scientists, the well-
trained ninja will need the ability to withstand severe temperatures
at both ends of the spectrum without getting hypothermia or a bad
sunburn.

Dresses and skirts: Mobile concealment is perhaps the most
difficult to master. To execute, plant yourself between a woman's legs.
As she moves, you must silently move with her, neither making a

noise, ruffling her dress or touching her skin. The skilled ninja can travel miles between a target's legs without being noticed or getting aroused.

✳ ✳ ✳

CAMOUFLAGE

The original human chameleons, ninjas have always incorporated their natural surroundings into the hunt. Fathers of several classic Japanese outfits, ninjas birthed such fashion trends as the high bamboo forest kimono, the ocean kelp jumpsuit and the trendy desert-chic look. Today, the most innovative urban clothing designers and full-body makeup artists are essential to the working ninja. Hiding in broad daylight can mean becoming a bush, blade of grass or prized Pinot Noir vine. In the city, the skilled ninja should be able to transform at a moment's notice from a graffiti-ravaged brick wall to a discarded IKEA dresser to a neon sign advertising *NUDE! NUDE! NUDE!*

To obtain the skills necessary to camouflage yourself, you must become versed in both makeup application and sewing. Start with a beginner's class in still life and landscape painting, and ask your mom for a quick stitching lesson. *Important Note:* When choosing paint for your body, remember to stay away from glitter-infused products, no matter how dazzling they may look.

When the sharpshooters of WWI began to construct gilly suits for a lifesaving camouflage edge outside the trenches, they turned to the famed Black Forest ninja clans for advice.

✳ ✳ ✳
DISGUISE

Masters of disguise, ninjas can hide *as humans* within mere feet of their targets. Originally used to spy on opponents and attain vital political information, ninjas would hide on the streets or in the cafés that their targets were known to frequent. On long-term espionage assignments, in which the ninja was hired to amass mountains of information on their target, ninjas would find ways to engage *directly* with the enemy. Masters of charisma and seduction, ninjas would often ingratiate themselves into their target's lives with a few furtive glances and suggestive caresses. Alternatively, uglier ninjas would become employees of their targets.

Male Disguises: The original male ninja disguises were fairly limited, ranging from wandering monk to merchant to traveling singer to beggar. As the ninja's foothold spread beyond the shores of Japan, their target demographics diversified, and they were forced to become more sophisticated. They expanded their repertoire to include more modern disguises, such as that of the urban thug or nondescript catalog model.

Female Disguises—*Kunoichi:* Ninja clans have always been equal opportunity employers. Unlike the sexist warriors of the Western world, early clans eagerly recruited women to become *kunoichi*, female ninjas. Capable of infiltrating enemy strongholds in ways no male warrior could, *kunoichi* warriors became invaluable to their clans and notoriously feared killers to their horny enemies. Traditionally, the *kunoichi* were trained primarily in the arts of espionage and close-

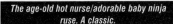
The age-old hot nurse/adorable baby ninja ruse. A classic.

range combat. Disguised as a scantily clad maid, a vivacious house cook or an irresistible geisha, *kunoichi* would use coquetry and charm to prey on a male target's primitive weakness, lust. Like their male counterparts, *kunoichi* disguises evolved with the times, and now *kunoichi* may don the garbs of a coquettish nanny, aggressive business-woman or hungover hipster on a fixie.

✳ ✳ ✳

DISTRACTION

The final element of *going unperceived* is the ninja's use of distraction. Well-trained in the area of cognitive neuroscience, ninjas would use an opponent's senses against them, diverting their attention with sounds, smells, optical illusions and dazzling ice sculptures. It's no wonder that David Copperfield calls the ninja "the first true magician."

Smoke Bombs: Smoke bombs are possibly the most essential item in any ninja's battle fanny pack. Filled with a smoky, gunpowdery mixture, smoke bombs, when thrown against a hard surface, will explode loudly, creating an auditory distraction, and form a thick, aromatic cloud of opaque milky-white smoke, creating both visual and olfactory distractions. However, smoke bombs are very difficult to find in your local firearms swap meets and weekend flash bang markets. If you're having trouble tracking down suitable supplies, try employing flares, M-80s or smoke grenades.

Blinding Powders: Blinding powders are concoctions that can be used to gain the advantage in a battle by temporarily marring an opponent's vision. Containing anything from hot peppers, wasabi and grapefruit juice for more benign uses to jellyfish poison, rattlesnake venom and wart juice to induce permanent damage, these concoctions are often delicious, but blinding powders can be also be quite painful and debilitating when thrown directly into an opponent's eyeballs.

Helpful Tip: If you are struggling with crafting a blinding powder with the right consistency, try adding a bit of baby powder. Easy on the hands and light, the baby powder will help deliver the stinging mixture as well as a jolt of childhood nostalgia. Modern alternatives include pepper spray and Windex.

Holograms and Advanced Technology: Always at the forefront of technology, most ninjas have begun to incorporate holograms, iPads, simple robots, and even 3-D flat-screen TVs to divert a target's attention.

Clones: Ninjas leave the moral implications of clone use to the experts, but many *ryu* have expressed a strong interest in creating clones of some of the most celebrated warriors.

CHAPTER 4

NINJA COMBAT
TECHNIQUES AND WEAPONS

*"Sticks and stones may break
my bones, but ninjas will always
kill me."*

—Japanese schoolyard saying

While *ninjutsu* emphasizes brain over brawn, the brain doesn't mean much if your body is a pear-shaped bag of disobedient brittle bones, saggy muscles and clogged arteries. Reshaping your body into a more traditional ninja shape and perfecting certain combat skills will make the difference between being the assassin and finding out what sort of afterlife is in store for mediocre ninjas like you.

You see, during your time as a professional ninja, you *will* get into several on-the-job fights. Whether on an espionage or assassination assignment or simply attempting to seduce the wrong person's sexual partner, chances are that you will find yourself in a violent confrontation during one of your first missions. While most of these battles will simply end with a few broken bones, bloody noses and/ or black eyes, a small percentage of them will be fought to the death.

It is this small percentage of fatal missions that has led the ninja to its place at the top of the list of America's most dangerous professions:

MOST DEADLY PROFESSIONS IN AMERICA

5. Sanitation Worker
Primary causes of death: Crushed by trash compactor
Rate: 37/100,000 employees

4. Construction Worker
Primary causes of death: Falls, tool-related disembowelments
Rate: 46/100,000 workers

3. Deep-Sea Fisherman
Primary causes of death: Drowning, shark bites, whale attacks
Rate: 129/100,000 fishermen

2. Mime
Primary causes of death: Audience revolt, mass psychotic breakdown
Rate: 1,956/100,000 actors

1. Ninja
Primary causes of death: Day-to-day life
Rate: 10,765/100,000 ninjas

But dying on the job need not be your destiny. Over the generations, ninjas have perfected several forms of martial combat, including weapons use (short-range, long-range, concealed); the striking arts (punching, kicking, head-butting); the grappling arts (pinning, take-downs, aggressive hugging) and a variety of one-strike death blows. As a ninja, it is imperative that you become a master of every aspect of *ninjutsu* combat.

The following is a breakdown of the most important traditional ninja combat techniques. With a mixture of history, proper technique and modern methods, this is arguably the most important part of this book, as it may well save your life.

Sometimes, grappling gets awkward.

✳ ✳ ✳

CLOSE-RANGE WEAPONRY

The striking and grappling arts force the ninja to risk injury by getting close to his opponent, and are therefore used only as a last resort. The ninja's first choice, of course, is long-range ninja weaponry, which allows the ninja to extinguish an opponent's life from afar. When long-range weaponry is not available, or when a ninja's opponent somehow manages to evade the long-distance assault, ninjas will resort to short-range combat weaponry.

WOODEN STAFFS: *BO, JO* AND *HAMBO*

These versatile ass-whooping sticks are the first weapons you should learn to utilize. Excellent tools for both defensive and offensive maneuvers, wooden staffs also make premium walking sticks for the long post-battle trek home. Choose your staff properly: The three-foot *hambo*, four-foot *jo* and six-foot *bo* each come with their benefits and drawbacks. For example, the lightweight *hambo* can easily be hidden in an airy pant leg, whereas the conspicuous *bo* is the optimum staff for smacking someone significantly out of arm's reach. Train with a wooden staff on a daily basis, and you should be able to target your opponent's vulnerable areas using "face blows," "back whacks," "leg swipes" and "ball rattlers."

Remember, the most painful strike you can deliver with a staff is with the beveled end. By concentrating the force of the blow into a reduced surface area, such a strike can easily shatter ribs, noses and modeling aspirations with a single jab.

When it comes to crafting your arsenal, Home Depot has a fantastic selection of strong wooden dowels that are ideal for training at home. If you can't find a suitable dowel, try training with a wooden mop handle or a pine two-by-four.

A ninja fights from roly-poly stance during a bo training.

A QUICK NOTE ABOUT BAMBOO

For centuries, hardy ninjas have used flexible stalks of bamboo for *bo* training. Lighter than traditional *bo* material, bamboo offers a cheap alternative and an excellent practice weapon. Home Depot offers a fantastic collection of dried pieces of bamboo in their "Ninja-Garden" section. Alternatively, starting your own mini-grove of this fast-growing giant grass is a great way to keep training costs down.

Size Doesn't Matter: Many ninjas have asked what to do when they find themselves swinging around a shamefully short shaft. Remember, it's not the size of your *hambo* that matters, but how well you thrust it at your opponent.

A ninja defends against a "Super Bo" attack.

NINJA-TO (SWORDS)

These simple, tough swords have been a ninja favorite for generations. Sharp in both design and material, and used in both battle and cookery, *ninja-to* can sever an opponent's head or slice the driest portions of a Thanksgiving turkey. *Ninja-to* pack neither the artful design nor the extraordinary strength of the exquisitely crafted samurai swords popular in Hollywood movies. Consider your *ninja-to* to be large, sharp, expendable knives rather than future family heirlooms.

Training with *Ninja-to*: The ninja sword's ultimate power lies in the quick jab rather than a saberlike swipe. When training your jab, it is best to first practice with juicy watermelons before you move on to stabbing sides of beef.

THE THREE S'S OF SAFE SWORD PLAY

When training your sword-fighting skills with a friend or fellow ninja, remember the all-important Three S's of Safe Sword Play: Slowly, Shallowly, Safely.

Slowly: Always practice your sword play at 95-percent speed, never at full speed.

Shallowly: Keep your stabs shallow. All practice stab wounds should be able to heal with minor surgery. No damage to vital organs!

Safely: No targeting eyes, testicles or gallbladders. Keep it safe and you'll keep it fun.

KUSARIGAMA (CHAINS)

The extremely dangerous *kusarigama* are a classic ninja example of using common household tools as ass-kicking battle gear. Simply a farming sickle suspended on a long, sturdy chain, the *kusarigama* can be used to stun targets from medium ranges or disembowel them with the sickle at close range. If you're planning on adopting the *kusarigama* outside of a traditional farming community, you should consider adapting the weapon for a more modern landscape. Since no one is going to buy your "I'm carrying my farming equipment to the field" excuse when you live in downtown Los Angeles, try a hip alternative like a bike lock, MacBook charger or designer handbag.

✵ ✵ ✵

CONCEALED WEAPONRY

You can't always carry a six-foot, blood-encrusted stick or a pair of razor-sharp steel swords in your day-to-day life. Concealed weaponry is vital to remaining heavily armed without drawing unwanted attention.

SHINOBI-ZUI (THE TRANSFORMABLE CANE)

The gentleman's cane may have gone out of style with the gramophone, but bringing a little dandy to your style could be a lifesaver. The *shinobi-zui,* a hollowed-out cane, is the perfect way to travel with a helpful selection of knives, chains and blow darts. If you can't imagine yourself pulling off the dapper look, try hollowing out a laptop, toy poodle or boom box for the same effect.

This evening stroll is about to get bloooody.

TANTŌ (DAGGERS)

The *tantō* is a must-have for the ninja making his or her way through daily life. Easy to conceal and an effective fighting weapon, a pair of *tantō* will ensure your safety in the most precarious situations. Keep your daggers taped securely to your inner thigh or tucked under your armpit when making your way through a crowded area. One of the reasons the *tantō* is so effective is that your assailant only finds out you have it when it's too late. Don't flash your daggers, use them to cut sandwiches or clean under your fingernails.

Fighting with sharpened *tantō* can be a bit intimidating, considering the close quarters needed for a successful defense. Fight in either "praying mantis" stance, with one blade protecting your forearm and the other poised for a forward stab; or in "rabid kitten" stance, with both blades wildly transitioning from one side to the other.

AIR TRAVEL WITH WEAPONRY

Commercial Airlines: Always pack all your steel weapons in your checked suitcase when traveling via commercial airlines. *Ninjair:* Ninjair carry-on policy has become stricter over the past few years, now limiting travelers to eight *shuriken* and 12 additional weapons.

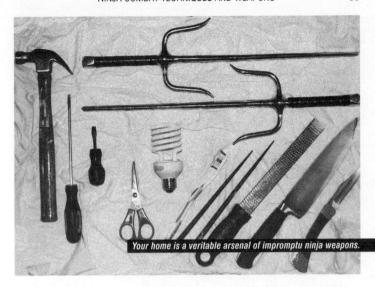

Your home is a veritable arsenal of impromptu ninja weapons.

✳ ✳ ✳
MID- AND LONG-RANGE WEAPONRY
SHURIKEN (THROWING BLADES)

Commonly known as "ninja stars," these intimidating throwing projectiles are an essential addition to your ninja satchel. Because of the short, two-inch blades, *shuriken* are generally not capable of delivering a lethal blow with the short two-inch blades. Instead, you should count on your *shuriken* to demoralize or stun an opponent rather than take them out. For safety, you should carry anywhere from eight to eighty *shuriken* on your body at all times (except through airport security). For best results in combat, you should plan on throwing a stack of three *shuriken* in each toss. During a battle, you may dispatch all of your *shuriken* before the fight is over. Fear not! The smart ninja can transform nearly any object, either sharp or blunt, into

A well-trained ninja should be capable of lethally flinging any utensil, not just multisided knives.

a decent *shuriken* replacement. Once you've perfected your triple-stack *shuriken* throwing technique, practice with objects found around the house, such as candelabras, coffee mugs or small pets.

YUMI (BOW & ARROW)

Arguably the most difficult weapon to master, the *yumi*, often called the Sniper Rifle of the East, is also considered the safest because it is the most accurate long distance weapon in the *ninjutsu* arsenal. By transferring a massive amount of energy into the high-speed arrow, the *yumi* is capable of delivering a deadly strike from distances of up to 500 yards. Chances are, your target won't know what's about to impale his neck before it's too late. The best ninja archers are equally accurate from a low crouch as they are from the back of a galloping horse. Today in America, the *yumi* has earned the somewhat unfortunate reputation of "lazy ninja's weapon" due to an embarrassing incident in which a poorly trained ANC attempted an assassination from his second story apartment. When the cops arrested him minutes later, he was still in his ninja Snuggie.

When training your stationary bow and arrow skills, do so at a formal archery range to prevent accidental impalements of family members and pets.

❊ ❊ ❊

FOOTWEAR AND CLIMBING GEAR

JIKA-TABI

Ninjas today still sport *jika-tabi*, the same style of footwear they donned in the era of the shogun. These split-toe boots resemble the type used for diving and surfing with Western wet suits. While affording little protection from sharp objects, the flexible shoes will aid your ability to climb ropes, trees and walls. Their soft, lightweight bottoms also ensure stealthy entry.

AISHIKI

To move from walls to ceilings, as well as up trees or telephone poles, you can strap on *aishiki*, small spikes that affix to the soles of your stylish *jika-tabi* shoes (much like Western crampons used in rock climbing). These metal spikes hinder ground movement and are about as difficult to remove as ski boots, so if you're faced with a quick climbing-to-running transition, make sure you have enough time to sit down and remove your spikes. If you can't get them off them in time, use your *aishiki* as a devastating kicking aid, sending the spikes into an exposed face or lightly clad reproductive organ.

SHUKU

Similar to *aishiki, shuku,* or "tiger claws," are worn on the hands to aid in climbing. Strapped around the wrist and palm with a thick piece of leather connecting the straps, the handgrips have two fanglike spikes that curve down from the fingers toward the forearm. While the grips make for superb climbing and a potentially painful open-hand slap, they will inhibit your ability to wield a sword and are dangerous if worn during a meal.

CHAPTER 5

HAND-to-HAND COMBAT

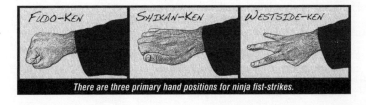

There are three primary hand positions for ninja fist-strikes.

For close-range, unarmed battles, you should be well trained in the grappling arts. By utilizing tackles, throws, holds and pins, a trained ninja who finds himself in a vicious scrap can completely immobilize his opponent with his body alone. Once immobilized, the ninja can choose from his varied arsenal of death blows, kill snaps and deadly smothers to terminate his opponent.

✳ ✳ ✳
STRIKING ARTS

The ninja, depending on his size, contours and bone density, can deliver a deadly blow with between 14 and 15 striking points (ninjas can kill opponents with either hand, elbow, knee, foot, shin and shoulder blade, or by striking with the forehead, chin or even nose). With his intimate knowledge of the human anatomy, the ninja aims to strike an opponent in one of his 49 target striking points. The following are the five most basic punches and kicks a ninja must know.

PUNCHES

***Zutsu* Jab:** Translated as the "hangover" jab, this is a quick, closed-fisted strike that leaves your opponent wondering what the *chin chin* just happened. Deliver your *zutsu* with your nondominant hand, saving your dominant hand for a more powerful knockout or death blow. As with all punches, most of the *zutsu*'s power comes from the ninja's shoulder and torso, rather than the arm itself. To deliver a powerful *zutsu* jab, take a small step forward with your front foot and lead your upper body toward your target with your shoulder as you strike. Remember to aim for the back of your opponent's brain rather than the surface of his face.

***Shuden* Uppercut:** Translated as "the last train uppercut," this savage punch is most often used to deliver a knockout blow. The *shuden* uppercut is most effective at close range and is a wise follow-up to a well-landed *zutsu* jab. To deliver the punch, bend your knees, coil your body and then unleash, aiming for your opponent's chin or solar

A ninja delivers a perfectly aimed guzu.

plexus; by rattling your opponent's brain, a chin strike will likely knock him out or at least cause him to see ninja stars.

***Guzu* Backhand:** The "lazy bitch" backhand is not physically debilitating so much as mentally demeaning. Best used in sure-win situations, the *guzu* is a humorous way to say to your opponent, "Who's the boss, *panku*?" A proper *guzu* should be delivered with as much nonchalance as you can muster.

***Tekuno* Chop:** Capable of shattering a pine board or a clavicle bone with one strike, the "techno" chop offers a sharp alternative to a punch. By channeling all of your power into the calcium-hardened outer edge of your hand, the *tekuno* chop delivers a more focused blow than a closed-fist punch. Aim for a vulnerable bone such as the clavicle, rib, forearm or cheekbone.

KICKS

Roundhouse: The roundhouse, an extremely versatile and powerful kick, can be used in almost any situation for both offensive strikes and to block an array of kicks. To execute the kick, begin at an angle to your opponent. Bring your leg into the air, rotate your hips toward your opponent and snap your leg at the knee, striking with the surface of your foot. Aim for the thigh, rib cage, face or jugular. *Note:* Westerners often confuse the simple roundhouse with the more flamboyant tornado.

Tornado: A favorite for all ninja fans, the tornado is the flamboyant ninja kick that incorporates raw power with a graceful spin. One of the most powerful nonweapon blows in the ninja's arsenal, the tornado is also a huge risk, as it momentarily leaves your back exposed. To execute the kick, bounce onto the ball of your right foot, spin quickly in a counterclockwise direction, plant your left foot and spring into the air, striking your opponent with the surface of your right foot.

Ball Rattler: A swift and sudden kick to the groin, the ball rattler is best executed when your opponent is a male who has passed through puberty. Not only will a well-aimed ball rattler leave your opponent in considerable pain, but it will also raise his voice a few octaves, making his smack-talking attempts hilarious for all parties involved.

Shin Masher: Used to quickly snap an opponent's tibia and bring him to the ground, the shin masher will give you a significant advantage over a foe by turning his leg into a shattered, floppy noodle. To execute the blow, lift your knee to your chest and then extend your foot down and out into your opponent's exposed shin.

Face Heel: Lift your knee to your chest and then extend your foot out and up, landing your heel directly in the face of your opponent. As with the *shuden* uppercut, the most effective face heel is one that lands squarely on your target's chin, rattling his brain and filling his vision with ninja stars.

✳ ✳ ✳

FIGHTING STANCES

After you've mastered basic stances such as Horse Stance, Forward Stance, and Cat Paw Stance, you'll need to learn to fight from the advanced karate and *ninjutsu* stances. Two of the most effective advanced stances are Playful Puppy Stance, which could save your life when you are forced to fight from the ground, and Champion's Stance, which allows you to deliver picture-perfect groin shots.

Playful Puppy Stance

Champion's Stance

✳ ✳ ✳

ADVANCED DEATH BLOWS

Ninjas have invented several ways of terminating an opponent with a single strike. Best used when an opponent has already been immobilized by one of the above-mentioned punches or kicks, advanced death blows are sure ways to end a battle and an opponent's life. While the following list is by no means complete (there are 16 death blows, so we've ignored the obvious ones, such as the Upward Nose Strike and the Neck Snap), it should illuminate the basic principles of delivering death blows.

The Ninja Master executes a blindingly accurate Enucleator during training.

The Enucleator (The Eye Gouge): A knuckle strike to the cheek may shatter an opponent's jaw, but a two-fingered eye gouge will render an opponent blind, possibly enucleated and, depending on the length of the ninja's phalanges, possibly brain-damaged or dead.

The Heart Squeeze: Depending on the ninja's fingernail calcium content and length, he may be able to penetrate his opponent's pectoral muscles and circumvent the rib cage, thereby reaching and squeezing the heart. This is a favorite of strong-phalanged ninjas, as it results in an opponent's instantaneous death.

The Lung Smother: Without the ability to breathe, an opponent will not be able to fight. During a well-aimed and forceful strike, ninjas can inject a poison or smothering particle-concoction into an opponent's lungs via the mouth. Deprived of oxygen, the opponent's brain will cease to function after two to four minutes (or about 28 minutes if the opponent is also a trained ninja).

�֍ �֍ ✖

KOPPOJUTSU
(THE ART OF BONE-BREAKING)

A heel jab to the femur, roundhouse kick to the rib cage or knuckle strike to the clavicle will result in a painful fracture and will weaken the opponent by immobilizing the area surrounding the break. While the human skeleton is generally regarded as rock hard, it is actually quite vulnerable to fractures and shatters. Most Americans have a low-calcium diet that results in flimsy, easily breakable bones, a weakness you cannot afford. Being able to withstand a rival ninja's *koppojutsu* moves is as important as knowing them yourself. Be sure to drink plenty of calcium-rich human breast milk and take calcium supplements and once-a-month Boniva to aid in bone density and strength.

✖ ✖ ✖

PRESSURE POINT FIGHTING

Ninjas identify the following 20 pressure points that, once struck, will fill an opponent with paralyzing pain. Learn the location and striking technique for each point so you can use it in battle:

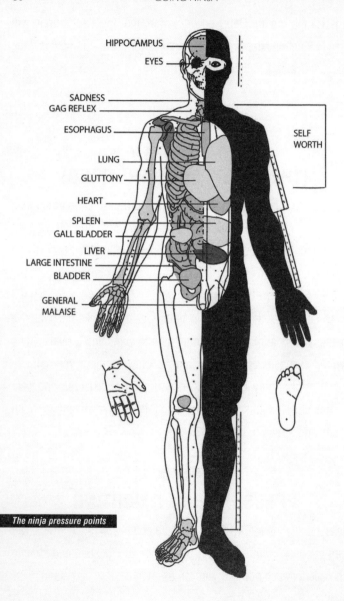

HIPPOCAMPUS

EYES

SADNESS
GAG REFLEX

ESOPHAGUS

LUNG

GLUTTONY

HEART

SPLEEN
GALL BLADDER

LIVER
LARGE INTESTINE
BLADDER

GENERAL
MALAISE

SELF
WORTH

The ninja pressure points

CHAPTER 6

MIND CONTROL
(ADVANCED)

Weapons, death blows, unarmed combat. So far, *ninjutsu* seems pretty savage, right? You haven't learned anything yet, young dragon.

The advanced ninja doesn't always deal in anything quite as low-brow as physical combat. As all ninjas must come to know, the mind is the most powerful weapon of all. And the ability to control an opponent's mind is the most deadly form of combat besides the strategically aimed nuclear warhead.

The average human is a slave to his emotions. Triggered by neural impulses, hormone imbalances and chemical secretions, emotions are mushy instincts, natural responses to external stimuli. Over the generations, ninjas have studied the human mind in agonizing detail, discovering the primary "emotional pressure points." Today, advanced ninjas know how to exploit this internal minefield with deadly precision.

Worldwide, the most effective ninjas are those who have learned the art of neurocontrol. Not only do these higher-order ninjas know how to control their own internal secretions, but, by combining a variety of chemical weapons with an equally varied array of physical tools, these superadvanced ninjas can control the minds—and therefore the behavior—of their opponents.

❋ ❋ ❋

INTERPERSONAL COMMUNICATION

To seal the bonds of friendship, humans utilize interpersonal cues such body language, comforting touch, kind facial expressions and extended eye contact. The ninja knows the average human's biological reaction to most interpersonal cues and can use them to manipulate a foe or lover in any number of fascinating ways.

EYE CONTACT AND FACIAL EXPRESSIONS

As a ninja, you should be able to easily communicate anger or kindness with a single glance, and you should likewise be able to induce fear or obsequiousness in an opponent with a prolonged stare. Remember, the following advanced moves will not be as effective when you are wearing your mask and are best utilized when you are disguised as a non-ninja.

The Puppy-Dog: Inducing pity in an opponent is one of the simplest ways to assure they do not attack. To execute the expression, form your mouth into a pout, wet your eyeballs so it appears as if you are tearing up and stare directly into your target's eyes. To induce extra-immobilizing tenderness, a believable lip quiver will easily take the Puppy-Dog to the next level.

The Suicide Inducer: The more advanced version of the puppy-dog stare, the Suicide Inducer is an expression so depressing that 90 percent of the people who witness it immediately take their own lives. *WARNING: Do not practice the Suicide Inducer in the mirror.*

The Sheep Killer: A move that combines snarled teeth, flared nostrils, a furrowed brow and bulged eyeballs, the well-executed Sheep Killer is an expression so frightening it will ignite every adrenal pathway in your victim, over-stimulating his heart and causing immediate cardiac arrest.

The You-Take-My-Breath-Away Smolder:
One of the most advanced moves in the ninja arsenal, the You-Take-My-Breath-Away Smolder is purported to be so sexy that it literally takes the victim's breath away, causing respiratory failure. Using a cute animal in conjunction with your own gaze will double the effect.

BODY LANGUAGE ASSAULTS

Often, a ninja's face is enshrouded behind his black *shinobi* mask. Without being able to fully utilize his face for a full facial expression attack, the ninja can still control an opponent's emotions with body language cues. For the most part, ninjas utilize body language assaults to injure an opponent mentally and/or physically without laying a finger on him.

Fake Punch: A well-executed Fake Punch will leave an opponent feeling as if he's actually been punched. The advanced ninja can deliver a fake punch from distances of up to 20 feet.

Withdrawn High-Five: The Withdrawn High-Five is a move used during battle to induce listlessness by leaving an opponent feeling unwelcome and friendless. To execute the technique, say something complimentary of your opponent, such as, "Nice punch, tiger," and then raise your arm into the classic pre-high-five position. At the last second, swing your palm out of your opponent's palm's trajectory, and say something demeaning like, "*Shitsukendayo*."

❊ ❊ ❊

NONVIOLENT PHYSICAL CONTACT

Contrary to popular belief, not all physical combat is violent. For the advanced ninja, a well-executed nonviolent move will be an effective immobilizer surpassing moves such as the tornado kick or *shuden* uppercut in effectiveness.

Massage: A soothing full-body deep-tissue oil massage can literally relax an opponent to death, slowing the heart rate so thoroughly that blood fails to reach the brain.

Mama Bear Hug: By giving an opponent a loving maternal hug, an advanced ninja can cause catatonia in an opponent by inducing a powerful cycle of nostalgia from which the victim has no chance of ever escaping.

Vicious Tickle: By targeting an opponent's anatomical "tickle points," a wily ninja can subdue a victim by causing him to laugh uncontrollably. A well-executed, prolonged Vicious Tickle will cause a victim to soil himself publicly and subsequently commit social *seppuku*.

HARNESSING THE UNIVERSE

Although it sounds a little hippy-dippy, the world's most deadly ninjas can manipulate the universe in two surprisingly wishy-washy ways. *Note*: The following moves are extremely advanced; only four ninjas worldwide possess the skills to properly execute them, so don't get frustrated if you aren't one of them.

The *Chi* Ball: By channeling his *chi*, the ninja can reshape the atoms available in the atmosphere into a compact, invisible ball and propel it into an opponent's gut, inducing instant death.

Bad Karma: By redistributing the universe's karma supply, the ninja can transfer deadly doses of bad karma to an opponent's soul, thereby assuring their "accidental" death some decades later.

USE SOMETHING LIKE:

Kill thee thy ~~tired~~ wicked,
thy evil, thy huddled
thieves. . .

other words to use:

sea-wash

Suns

Nir

Lightni

air-bridg

awesor

flar

stab-wound.

Part Two:
The American Ninja

Original 1864 drawing of the proposed Statue of Liberty, with notes.

CHAPTER 7

RED, WHITE AND BLOOD

"Like the swift eagle has accepted the waddling penguin as a fellow bird, so must we ninjas accept the American as member of the order of shinobi."

—Hiro Matsumi, Head of the GNF (Global Ninja Federation), in his famous speech "Let them In," delivered in Iga Togo, Japan, in May 2000

For decades, the stereotypical American has been seen as the polar opposite of the ninja. As a society, Americans have been construed as the sweaty, humid day to the ninja's sweet, cool night; the sludgy viscosity to their effervescent gaseousness. But appearances, like the wily ninja, can be deceiving. And despite the stark contrast and apparent incompatibility of lifestyles, hundreds of Americans are going ninja every day.

✳ ✳ ✳

A NINJA'S FUTURE
IN THE UNITED STATES

*Gone are the days when ninjas roamed
the prairies from Oklahoma to Okinawa.*

The tides of change are raging in America. Decades of overindulgence have left Americans gravitating toward a more austere way of life. In addition, 10 years of brutal military engagements have created a generation of battle-hardened veterans searching for something else to fight for.

While *ninjutsu* and its practitioners have pervaded the American consciousness for generations, it is only within the last couple of decades that *going ninja* has become a popular and common practice.

Despite the growing ninja culture in America, it wasn't until famed ninja Hiro Matsumi's controversial "Let Them In" speech, delivered to the Global Ninja Federation in Iga Togo, Japan, that American Ninjas were truly accepted into the global ninja community and recognized as actual ninjas.

....

THE AMERICAN NINJA CONVERT (ANC): 10 QUICK FACTS

1. In 1950, there were 211 ANCs; by 2000, that number had increased to 7,568; and by 2010, the American ninja numbers had swelled to 365,472.

2. Ninety percent of Americans become ninjas between the vulnerable ages of 18 and 29.

3. Sixty-seven percent of ANCs are male.

4. Converting to ninja costs an average of $20,500. The breakdown—weapons and ninja gear: $4,500; combat/fitness training: $2,000; espionage-related ninja cosmetics: $1,500; wardrobe purchases for disguises: a whopping $12,500.

5. Since 2005, unsolved murders in America have increased by 7 percent.

6. Almost all (98 percent) of ANCs were unmarried at the time of conversion.

7. Many ANCs (77 percent) were unemployed at the time of conversion.

8. The average ANC earns $180,000 annually from ninja services; however, this statistic is skewed by a handful of highly successful ninjas; the real median income is about $17.50 per hour.

9. While still vulnerable to recessions and economic down turns in the U.S., ninja-related jobs are ranked alongside nursing, education and technology as the first professions to recover.

10. On average, ANC professionals enjoy 9.25 weeks of paid vacation annually.

....

✹ ✹ ✹

WHY GO NINJA?
A CASE FOR CONVERSION

These days, it's hard to walk down the street without bumping into another American ninja convert. Not since 1967's Summer of Love saw millions become hippies has America's youth flocked so freely to a truly alternative lifestyle choice. But what are the underlying causes of this massive social exodus, why is it happening now, and what is the strongest case for going ninja?

AN EARLY LIFE CRISIS

For most young Americans, their life path has three branches: a life of drugs and crime, white-collar banality or the way of the ninja. Considering the options, it's no surprise that going ninja is becoming so prevalent among young American adults that many sociologists are referring to the "Millennials" as "Generation *Yakitori*."

The most prevalent cause of going ninja for Generation *Yakitori*, according to a recent census of ANCs, is an occurrence known as the quarter-life crisis. Unique to wealthy Western societies and a relatively recent phenomenon, the quarter-life crisis is considered by experts to be a consequence of poor—or at least misleading—baby boomer parenting techniques.

"As parents, most baby boomers have adopted especially supportive parental styles, a subconscious act of rebellion against their own constrictive upbringing," writes ninja expert James Remault, a visiting professor of sociology at Florida State Ninja University in an essay. "Children have been taught to follow their dreams and believe they can be whatever they desire to be. As a result, you have a generation of twentysomethings who can't possibly understand why they aren't successful actors, musicians, Crayola artists, bestselling humor writers or celebrated chefs. *Ninjutsu* is the perfect way for these young adults to achieve independence and be involved professionally in an 'art,' even if that art is the art of assassination."

THE ECONOMY

Over the past few years, the U.S. has seen an economic collapse rivaled in American history only by the Great Depression. While "things are *futeki* all over," American college graduates aged 22 to 37 have reported more cases of acute "recession depression" than any other demographic.

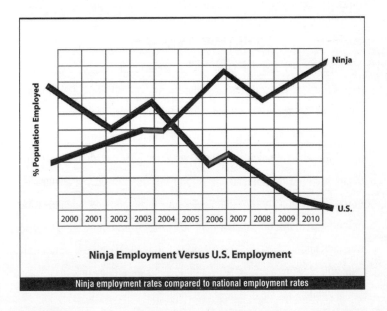

Ninja Employment Versus U.S. Employment

Ninja employment rates compared to national employment rates

"Ninja services are in greater demand than ever," explains Marshall Donovan, an American ninja convert. "In any recession," he says, "more people get fired or demoted by bosses, dumped or cheated on by lovers, or out-hustled by rivals. In this growing climate of anger and frustration, I've been getting an assassination assignment nearly every week!"

SEX

A large contingent of American ninjas has gone ninja for largely superficial reasons—specifically the perceived sexiness of the black hood and phallic weaponry. However, this ridiculous goal of sexual gratification is rarely achieved because a primary tenant of ninjaism is secrecy; once these converts realize that they can't say to hot girls, "Want to see the inside of my dojo?" they find themselves back in the same ocean of salty loneliness they were drifting in before conversion.

LIFESTYLE AND HEALTH

Although many people convert for superficial reasons, an equal proportion of converts makes the move out of legitimate health concerns. As America fattens up on burgers and deep-fried pizzas, overweight citizens are turning to the now-famous Ninja Battle Diet as a natural alternative to questionable weight-loss diets and detox cleanses. First revealed to the public in 2009, the Ninja Battle Diet burns fat as quickly and effectively as the Atkins Diet, cleanses the colon more thoroughly than the Master Cleanse and builds finely toned muscles faster than a juicing meathead. The Ninja Battle Diet not only gets you fit, ripped and healthy, but does so with many delicious meal choices such as rice and uncooked barley.

SOCIAL STATUS

The desire to be cool has led to a number of recent ninja conversions. Specifically, many Americans believe they can jump a few rungs on the social ladder once they learn a few basic ninja tricks or assassinate a couple dozen people. This belief, for the same reason as the "ninjas are sexy" assumption, has been almost uniformly false. With a need for secrecy, ANCs cannot simply go into a bar and perform ninja tricks. Furthermore, that same ANC cannot go into a bar and brag about his most recent assassination, unless he wants to get arrested. For these reasons, most Americans who go ninja for an elevated social status find themselves as unpopular as ever.

However, as converts become more comfortable with their ninja skills, they learn how to display their newfound talents in socially acceptable ways and without revealing their identities. By destroying the opposition in popular bar games such as beer pong, darts and lawn bowling, several ninjas have catapulted themselves to the top of their social ladder without exposing themselves. Likewise, the more subtle ninja converts have begun to use their espionage skills to ascertain important pieces of gossip about rival cool people; they then spread said pieces of gossip like wildfire, thus toppling their rivals.

✤ ✤ ✤

FREQUENTLY ASKED QUESTIONS

The fact that you picked up this book shows that you have a serious interest in becoming a ninja. But the path to ninjahood, as surely you know, is fraught with peril, immense physical pain, mental torture, hours of intense games of chess and badminton, gallons of spilled blood, meters of disemboweled intestines and, perhaps least desirably of all, millions of grains of plain white rice, sans soy sauce.

So is it worth it, you ask? Is the outcome worth the trials and tribulations of the journey? What are the end results?

Slow down, young grasshopper, soon enough. Time rushed is time more quickly lost.

WILL I WIN FIGHTS?

Yes. But fighting is not the answer. This is not a book on Israeli krav maga, Brazilian jiu-jitsu or Algerian death tickling. We are not teaching you to be a testosterone-driven brute. *Ninjutsu* will teach you both combat and espionage so you will be capable of beating the crap out of foes and making a clean escape. But heed this warning; the days of the violent ninja are past. Most modern ninjas claim to be active pacifists, using their combat skills to deter fights rather than start them, saving their weapons to intimidate rather than eviscerate.

The true power of the ninja lies not in the thrust of his sword or the spike of his well-aimed *shuriken*, but in the power of his charisma and the prickle of his cleverly worded insults.

WILL I BE SEXY?

Because of this peaceful paradigm shift, ninjas are becoming more positively regarded in certain circles. In fact, the ninja is ranked just below rock stars and slightly above firemen in *GQ* magazine's "List of Sexiest Professions," while as recently as the 1990s they were ranked behind pig farmers on the very same list. The perceived sexiness of the ninja can be attributed to a number of physical factors, notably their sinewy, rippling musculature, calcium-rich unbreakable bones, mysterious stares and flexible limbs.

WILL I BE RICH?

Remember what Buddha says: "What is more money but a handful more problems?"

While the most successful ninjas can earn millions of dollars annually, most ninjas earn modest salaries ranging from $10,000 to $40,000 each year. Moreover, during your initial training you will be significantly poorer. Because you will spend most of time perfecting somersaults, advanced walking techniques and other ninja moves, your performance at your day job will suffer, and you will probably be fired. What will follow will be a seriously impoverished period in your life, and you will be probably not be able to afford any sake.

TOP TEN NINJA BENEFITS

1. Ninjas are never afraid of the dark, for they can see with their noses and ears.

2. Ninjas have complete control over their bladders and therefore never have to urinate at inconvenient times.

3. Ninjas have stomachs that ripple like a thousand pebbles thrown in a still lake.

4. Despite eating 17 meals per day, ninjas have only 2 percent body fat.

5. Thanks to flexible work schedules, ninjas never have to commute during rush hour traffic.

6. Ninjas are 22 percent less likely than non-ninjas to experience tooth decay, male-pattern baldness or athlete's foot.

7. Even the most emotional ninja has enough self-control to deter Girl Scouts and not buy their cookies.

8. Though ninjas are not slaves to their sexual urges, they still get laid 42 times more often than the average American non-ninja.

9. The ninja, on average, lives to be 137 years old.

10. Ninjas can do extremely impressive handstands.

TOP TEN NINJA DRAWBACKS

1. Ninjas are not eligible for Social Security.

2. Marriage between a ninja and a non-ninja is *not* allowed in 47 states.

3. Murder is illegal in the United States and it's punishable by execution, jail time, community service or, worse, all of the above.

4. Despite having easy access to some of the greatest fast-food chains in the world, American ninjas must avoid the temptation of a juicy burger at all times.

5. Whenever someone gets killed with a bow and arrow, the "maim-stream media" inevitably blames the ninja.

6. The traditional black outfits are stylish and chic, but unbearably hot during the dog days of summer.

7. Ninjas must not slay children on Halloween, despite having their characteristic style mocked by undisciplined trick-or-treaters across the country.

8. During times of peace and prosperity, the need for assassination-related services is often depressed.

9. Ninjas are more commonly prone to gingivitis than non-ninjas are.

10. Ninjas, being deep philosophers, are terrible at small talk.

CHAPTER 8

AMERICAN IDLE:
THE NINJA TRANSITION BEGINS

"Walk quickly. Chew no gum.
Do push-ups. Carry sharpened
swords."

—Yuki Katsura, from *A Guide to Western Ninja*,
published 1984

❄ ❄ ❄

INITIAL PHYSICAL TRAINING:
THE FIRST WEEK

As you know, *ninja* is synonymous with "ass-kicking badass," and
while *ninjutsu* literally means "the art of stealth," it is sometimes
translated as "the art of kicking ass and taking names." Yes, combat
training is an integral part of any ninja's upbringing, so much so that

ninja experts have used words like "vital," "magnanimous" and, of course, "the bee's knees" when asked to describe physical training's relative importance along the path to ninjahood.

In fact, a recent study found that the average Japanese ninja's training regimen consisted of 160 hours per week of physical training, a number that doubles for teenage ninjas. Unfortunately for you, our dear Western reader, achieving sustained activity for such time may prove fatal, or at least incompatible with your television-viewing habits.

Instead of jumping into the deep end of ninja physical training, try waiting 30 minutes to digest your meal, then test the waters of the kiddy pool to make sure it's not too chilly for your delicate skin.

Don't go from an average American life (desk job, alcoholism, Arby's) straight into a typical 160-hour-per-week training regimen; instead make your transition slowly, in increments, so that your body may accustom itself over two or even three weeks to the rigorous schedule. Moreover, there's no reason to quickly abandon the activities that you've enjoyed for your entire life; instead, take normal, everyday activities such as television viewing, texting, eating and recreating, and incorporate them into your training routine.

✳ ✤ ✳

STARTING NINJUTSU COMBAT:
BASIC KARATE

The first step toward becoming an ideal physical specimen is to join your local karate dojo and take advantage of their complimentary beginner lessons. If you have taken your initial mental training

TALES OF AN
ASPIRING AMERICAN NINJA, PART 1

Subject: Evan P., male

Ninja Name: Clarence of the Skinny Jeans

Age: 27

Location: Brooklyn, NY

Former Occupation: Computer Technician

Shortly after turning 26 years of age, subject Evan P. reportedly suffered a quarter-life crisis. Until then, he had led what he considered to be a successful—if not happy—life. Employed as a computer tech, he had a pretty girlfriend with whom he shared an apartment and trips to the farmer's market on Saturdays. It was a life of peace. But it was not enough.

When Evan decided to take the leap and become a ninja, he was not prepared for the physical transformation required of him. Despite being relatively self-disciplined and a decent squash player, Evan's physical fortitude had atrophied during years of American idleness.

Like most modern young urbanites, Evan's solution was to get in shape by cruising the streets of Brooklyn on a single-speed bike while making frequent stops at record stores, bookshops and art galleries. The regimen hardly prepared him for ninjahood, and when he was allowed to audition for a local ninja clan, he was promptly defeated by the clan's weakest member in a game of pin the tail on the starving tiger.

Lesson: Train harder.

seriously, one or two classes should be enough for you to absorb all the karate techniques necessary. And while it is true that most of your karate classmates will be under the age of 12, with markedly childlike frames, rest assured the situation will be challenging. If you are at least moderately strong, you will gain an essential ninja self-assurance by beating the crap out of young children who are so much weaker than you are.

If you decide to continue with your karate lessons, you will trade in your white belt for one with a more yellowish hue, and this tremendous step will make you overflow with confidence. So, tarry not—put down this book and go sign up!

This kid is 4'2", weighs 64 pounds and will hand you the beating of your lifetime.

✻ ✻ ✻
NINJA RUNNING

Karate will begin to shape your muscles and initiate you to the world of combat, but as many ninja missions require quick chase downs or long hunts that can last many days and several thousand miles, you will need to train your body to run for both speed and distance. Here's a suggested jogging schedule:

Day 1: 0.5 mile / *target time:* 20 minutes

Day 2: 1 mile / *target time:* 20 minutes

Day 3: 5 miles / *target time:* 20 minutes

Day 4: 10 miles / *target time:* 20 minutes

Day 5: Rest

Day 6: Marathon for a Cure / *target time:* 21 minutes

RUNNING WITH SCISSORS/SHARPENED KNIVES

Often enough, the ninja must defend and attack using deadly weapons while running. This art of high-speed multitasking is tough to master and takes serious practice. To begin, try running while holding items like MP3 players, water bottles or twigs—anything that will impale neither you nor passersby during your public sprints. Once carrying these items feels natural, move on to ones that take a bit more concentration: Try eating a sandwich or enjoying an ice cream cone while running. Then take the next step to scalding liquids like coffee or bacon grease. After that, running with sharpened knives or swords should be a breeze.

Always remember to stay hydrated and monitor your heart rate.

MARATHON FOR A CURE FOR STAB WOUNDS

Over the past few years, the nonprofit ninja organization *Race for a Red Miracle* has hosted ninja marathons in Chicago, New York, Boise and Los Angeles. All donations help fund the development of a cure for stab wounds—a horrific condition that affects almost seven of every ten ninjas in America. So put your training to the test for a good cause!

✳ ✳ ✳

NINJA STRENGTH TRAINING

ARMS AND BACK

When training to be a *ninjutsu* warrior, you should focus on muscle stamina rather than bulk. Doing more repetitions with lighter weights means smaller, but more explosive, muscles. The following regimen will get you to peak strength without sacrificing quickness.

Biceps Curls (10 sets of 100 reps per day): Known as the glamour muscles, a pair of sinewy biceps will not only impress the ladies but it will help you pack more of a punch into your punch. When doing biceps curls, hold the weight in your hand and bring it slowly from your hip to your shoulder, keeping your upper arm and back perfectly still.

Pull-ups (500 per day): When it comes to a well-rounded strength-training exercise, pull-ups take the cake. A proper pull-up will work over 60 muscles, including your biceps, triceps, forearms, upper back, lower back and stomach, and will eventually give your body that sexy *V* shape you've always wanted by stretching your latissimus dorsi into a sinewy, *soba* noodle–shaped thing of strength and beauty.

On-the-Go Alternative—Aggressive High Fives and Handshakes (several thousand per day): A favorite American pastime is the testosterone-filled physical greeting. The overly strong handshake and painfully hard high five are ageless examples of this showy alpha-dog behavior. Take it to the next level: A good American ninja-in-training will execute handshakes and high fives throughout the day with friends, strangers and bus drivers alike, utilizing several hundred upper-body muscles each time.

CHEST AND NECK

A powerful set of pectoral muscles is necessary for a well-executed cartwheel, and a strong, sinewy neck is even more vital. During battle, your opponent may target your jugular. A strong-enough neck can deter most roundhouse kicks, *tekunu* chops and even some poorly constructed swords.

Bench Press (10 sets of 100 per day): This classic exercise will enlarge your pectorals in both a sexy and useful way. A powerful chest is necessary for the grappling arts but will also help you during espionage missions by giving you the strength to remain hidden in unnatural positions for hours or even days on end. To execute a bench press, find a weight or a chubby person, hold them above your chest with your arms tucked in, then fully extend your arms.

The Swan Swivel (1,000 per day): This is a simple but challenging exercise; to execute, stretch your neck upward as high as you are able, and then slowly rotate your head as far to the left as possible; hold for 20 seconds, then rotate it as far right as possible and hold for 20 seconds. A disciplined swan swivel routine will have the dual effect of strengthening your neck and increasing its dexterity, which will allow you to see and hear in all directions.

LEGS AND CORE

The core—which includes your lower back, stomach, buttocks and upper thighs—is the most important part of a ninja's body. While most strikes come from your feet, shins or hands, most of the power actually generated in your core. Having a strong core means having a strong attack. Furthermore, a strong core will help you achieve good balance, which will enable you to stay on your feet on both the battlefield and the dance floor!

Side Note: The buttocks, on any normally shaped human, are the largest muscles. Having large and sturdy buttocks is essential for walking, lunging, kicking, jumping, landing and pretty much any physical activity you can think of.

Squats (4 sets of 25 reps, twice daily): Having strong thighs is vital for kicking powerfully, landing excessive jumps and maintaining balance during a battle. Strengthening your thighs is achieved through weighted squats. To execute a proper squat, hold something heavy above your shoulders (a couch or small tiger), then squat, bringing your buttocks toward your heels. To assure that your power is coming from your thighs, make sure to keep your back as straight as possible.

Sit-ups (1,000 per day): A proper sit-up regimen will not only give you that rippling stomach you've always desired but also hone almost every attack muscle. When executing a proper sit-up, do it slowly and sensuously to assure that your stomach and lower back—rather than your upper back—are doing the bulk of the work.

On-the-Go Alternative—The "Turkish Latrine" (1 to 12 times per day): Most Americans engage in mindless bathroom reading while performing their daily constitutionals. Most ninjas, on the other hand, utilize defecation to strengthen their core muscles. Instead of sitting comfortably on the toilet, squat on the seat in order to work your thigh and lower core muscles. This "Turkish latrine" workout is an easy one to do every day.

✳ ✳ ✳

NINJA HAND-EYE COORDINATION

Having strength means nothing if you don't know how to direct it. In combat, you cannot afford to miss your target by an inch. Being a skilled ninja means having precise control over your muscle movements. Sure, a *hambo* strike to an opponent's kneecap allows for a certain amount of imprecision, but shooting a moving opponent in the neck with an arrow from half a mile's distance requires extreme concentration and precision. Anything less than immaculate hand-eye coordination *will* result in your death.

TAKKYU (DEATHBALL)

The ninja bar game of choice has always been *ninjutsu takkyu* (deathball; known in the States as "Ping-Pong" or "table tennis"). In the 15th century, the training regimen of preteen and teenage ninjas included 20 hours weekly of Ping-Pong, which was considered the ultimate way to improve hand-eye coordination. Traditionally, balls were dipped into a cauldron of neurotoxins; the game would end only once one player managed to sneak the poisoned ball into his opponent's mouth, hence coining the term "kill shot."

Helpful Tip: *Do not* play Ping-Pong in pants. Get a pair of very small shorts to ensure both mobility and an authentic look.

Giant kobutori flies are ideal for beginners.

CHOPSTICK TRAINING

Popularized in *The Karate Kid,* the ancient ninja training technique of fly-catching is still a common way to develop hand-eye coordination. Unfortunately, most Americans are mediocre chopstick users at best, so you may want to begin by snagging sushi off a slow-moving sushi boat before moving on to insects.

❄ ❄ ❄

AGILITY, FLEXIBILITY AND BALANCE
GOAT STANCE

If you're a martial-arts film buff, chances are you've seen many a fighting master practicing the majestic strikes, kicks and poses of goat stance. Based on the movements of the incredibly agile, remarkably flexible Mongolian house goat, this stance incorporates yoga-style flexibility with gymnastic acrobatics and a flurry of awkward limb strikes. Goat stance is among the most efficient ways to increase strength, flexibility and balance at once.

YOGA

Yoga is not just for hippies and yuppies. This combination of exercise and mediation will increase your flexibility and dexterity and give you that everimportant mental cooldown you will need after a hard-fought battle or taxing assassination attempt. Ninjas have been practicing variations of yoga since their days in the mountains of Japan, and many claim that a lifelong routine will add decades to your lifespan.

TWISTER

Twister has been the best-selling recreational game in Japan since the late 17th century for a reason. Utilizing several muscles and honing agility, flexibility and balance at once, and socially acceptable amidst non-ninjas, Twister is considered an integral part of any ninja's training regimen. Challenge your friends and coworkers to a game every chance you get. And when you're good enough, you may want to fill the white space between the colored circles with sharp, rusty nails without updating your tetanus vaccination.

POLE DANCING

American ninjas have been engaging in competitive pole dancing for generations. With difficult moves like the Swirling Rattlesnake, the Disobedient Dragon and, of course, the Inebriated Marsupial, it's no wonder pole dancing is considered a prime way to improve agility, flexibility and balance while having a blast! Furthermore, once you graduate to actual ninja status, a well-performed striptease may be an excellent way to subdue and distract a target before you attack. Every ninja-in-training should install a pole in their primary residence.

✳ ✳ ✳

SIMPLE LIFESTYLE CHANGES TO MAKE TODAY

The Sake Switcheroo: Like to enjoy a couple brewskies when the work day winds down? Stop immediately! Most beers contain unhealthy doses of empty calories, which will stymie your physical training by making you fat around the middle. Switch to unfiltered extralight sake, the beverage of the demigods and lesser saints.

Sleeping: Training at all times means training at all times, including while sleeping. Because the average ninja assassination lasts 36 hours, you must learn to sleep while balanced in precarious places. As such, you must slumber in a variety of foreign sleeping locales and positions, including atop telephone polls, stuffed into washing machines and/or dryers, balanced on tree branches and, of course, while engaged in a handstand.

Sprint, Don't Walk: When getting from point A to point B, most Americans partake in the "Western stroll," a lazy, slow-paced walk. The aspiring ninja, however, must eliminate walking from his daily routine and replace it with quick speed bursts. Whether going to the corner store for a burrito, heading up the stairs to bring your mother a mug of herbal tea or heading to the movie theaters with a new date, you must incorporate in sprints into every jaunt.

Driving: Driving is time-consuming, but it can also be a great training opportunity. Because *ninjutsu* utilizes 14 to 15 striking points, you should train and strengthen all of them while driving by steering and accelerating using every possible striking-point combination. Some examples include: steer with your knee while accelerating with your shoulder blade; or accelerate with your chin and steer with your nose. This training exercise also hones the proximal sense; because you face will not necessarily be positioned properly, you must "see" the road with your ears and nostrils.

CHAPTER 9

LEARNING
TO READ
JAPANESE

Every official ninja is required to obtain an elementary understanding of the Japanese language, both spoken and written. Unfortunately for most Americans, the concept of learning to read an alien language like Japanese is more difficult than mastering quantum calculus. What most aspiring American ninjas don't realize is that Japanese, along with Mandarin Chinese, are the two easiest written languages in the world to pick up.

How is that possible? Emoticons, that's how.

The Greek alphabet and its lingual descendants (including our modern English Latin-based alphabet) are logographic, using symbols to represent *sounds*. Japanese kanji, on the other hand, is an *emoticon*-based written language, meaning that each symbol directly portrays a feeling, object, action, place or person. Reading kanji is simply about learning to identify the items drawn before you. For example:

COMMON THINGS

図   Drawing

品   Take-out containers

自   Trash bin

心   Happy face

食   Ski cabin

入   Tsunami

COMMON ACTIVITIES

 Happy hour   Surfing

 Skydiving   Stabbing

Now try for yourself! Decipher the following simple kanji characters:

曜 _____

委愛験 _____

考親 _____

CHAPTER 10

NINJAS AND THE
SEVEN DEADLY SINS

As discipline is a vital part of any ninja's success, the American who wishes to go ninja must learn to be utterly self-disciplined at all times. During the first month of your transition, this aspect of training will be by far the most painful and difficult.

In ancient Japan, the ninja recognized five essential weaknesses in humans (anger, sympathy, greed, fear and lust), but Westerners are mentally infantile compared to ninjas and actually have *seven*. So called because they bring about spiritual death, the seven deadly sins have also brought about physical death in many a weak-spirited American ninja. To become an excellent ninja, you must rid yourself of pride, covetousness, lust, anger, gluttony, envy and even sloth.

Pride: As the saying goes, there is no *I* in *ninja*. For the aspiring ninja, pride is the single most debilitating of the sins because anonymity is the only way to survive a lifetime under the black mask. You will never get recognition or receive accolades for your ninja work. During your missions as a ninja, your personality will be smothered underneath a matryoshka doll of aliases and alternate personalities used for disguises. The ninja with a large ego always exposes his true self during a mission, a mistake which leads so many ninja mothers to outlive their ninja children.

Covetousness: This is perhaps the hardest of the seven to extinguish, because most Americans haven't the slightest clue what it means, and even those who do aren't sure how it's any different from envy. The trick to eliminating covetousness from your person is to learn the definition.

Lust: Don't worry—by no means is the ninja forbidden from having intercourse or engaging in sexual activity. After all, isn't that half the reason you wanted to become a ninja in the first place? However, skilled ninjas will always organize sexual encounters to accommodate their schedule, never engaging in copulation at a lover's or seductress's behest. To train yourself in the art of sexual control, allow yourself only one wet dream per month.

Anger: As the catchy saying goes, "The ninja provoked to anger is the ninja who is stabbed in the abdomen with a sharp sword and dies a slow and painful death." As such, it is vital that you learn to completely sublimate any feelings of anger or its petty cousins umbrage and perturbation. To do so, ask your family and friends to gang up on you, constantly assaulting you with a barrage of angering, annoying, or resentment-inducing remarks.

Gluttony: To cow your Western gluttony into utter submission, you must arrange for constant temptations in front of your nose at all times. Place plates of freshly baked chocolate chip cookies and bowls of Lucky Charms throughout your house, and carry burritos and nachos in your pocket or purse at all times. Whenever you submit to your desires, stab yourself shallowly with a serrated knife. In this way, you will learn to control your desires through negative association.

Envy: As the good book says, "Thou shall not envy others, lest thou wanteth be striketh down with a killer bolt of lightning." The only way rid your mind of envy is by completely desensitizing yourself to it by inciting it in the most painful ways. For example, if you are given a delicious burrito, hand it to a random person on the street and watch them make ravenous mouth love to it until your envy is but a doused coal in the blackened hearth of your soul.

Sloth: The crown of thorns that sits atop the heads of most Americans, sloth, or slothfulness, is the most debilitating of the seven sins. To purge yourself of the disease of laziness, you must sever it from its source—television and the Internet. Smash your TV screen with a metallic baseball bat and slice your Ethernet cable with a box cutter. Now when boredom strikes, you will reach for your training knives, running shoes or instructional books instead of the remote or mouse. *Important Note:* Remember, once you've passed through the transition phase and become a GNC sanctioned ninja, you will want to reinstall your Internet for marketing, networking and socializing purposes.

CHAPTER 11

CONTINUING NINJA TRANSITION AND TRAINING

Congratulations, you're well on your way to actual ninja status! You've spent a couple grueling weeks engaged in beginning ninja training, learning basic elements of *ninjutsu* and exploring the diverse pleasures of sake. You've grown muscles where you once had pockets of air, become fractionally more attractive to the opposite sex and have probably had a pretty good time doing these things!

But being a ninja isn't all fun and games. In fact, in many ways the ninja's life is tougher and more painful than the average American's. You may feel alienated at times. Because you are better than almost everyone else, it will be hard to make friends or lovers who you find worthy of your time, and because of your nomadic job, it will be difficult to maintain a stable family life. Furthermore, ninjas are an extreme political minority. In fact, in a recent survey only three White House representatives said they would vote for a bill that would legalize marriages between ninjas and non-ninjas. In the southern states, ninjas are not even recognized as citizens.

Do not despair; this book is a comprehensive guide for the aspiring ninja. Not only does it detail the process of becoming an expert ninja, it also identifies and presents viable solutions to virtually all roadblocks and obstacles that you will encounter during your life.

✳ ✳ ✳

COMING OUT AS A NINJA

If you're still reading this book, chances are you've decided that there's a ninja inside of you that's been waiting to surface for your entire life. The next step is to reveal your true identity to your friends and family.

COMING OUT TO YOUR FATHER: AN EXPERT STEP-BY-STEP GUIDE

1. Do it in a public forum, such as a restaurant or a sporting event, so that he will not make a scene.

2. Make sure he is sitting; he may faint.

3. Look him in the eyes with a look that says *"kono kusottare!"*

4. Say, "Dad, I am a ninja," in a soft, soothing voice. Touch his hand.

5. Assure him that you are still you.

6. Show him a few of your best ninja moves. For example, do a really excellent somersault. If you have the skills, you may even want to try a cartwheel.

While opening the door of the ninja closet is always painful, following these steps will make the process easier for you and your loved ones. Though the steps will vary slightly depending on whom you are coming out to, the basic principals remain the same. The three most important aspects of coming out are showing off your ninja skills, possibly exercising some bone-shattering *koppojutsu* if the person takes the news poorly, and being gentle and open about what you have decided.

✳ ✳ ✳

NINJA PREJUDICES

If ninjas are one thing, they are bad-ass killers. But if they are another thing, they are misunderstood. While ninjas have historically been accepted, respected, and even, in some cases, idolized, in modern America the ninja is as hated and judged as the most disenfranchised minorities. Consequently, once you've revealed your true identity to the world, you will encounter hate, prejudice, mockery, alienation and a whole litany of sadnesses that truly suck. The one piece of good news is that hate crimes against ninjas pretty much never happen.

TOP TEN MOST FEARED/HATED GROUPS IN AMERICA

10. Clowns	5. Democrats
9. Pool cleaners	4. Republicans
8. Residents of New Jersey	3. Parking enforcement officers
7. **Ninjas**	2. Terrorists
6. IRS agents	1. Mimes

Always remember, your career choice could have been worse.

SOURCES OF ANTI-NINJA SENTIMENT

To dampen the hate you will encounter as a ninja, it is paramount that you understand the nature and source of the anti-ninja bigot and his prejudices. America's unfavorable view of the ninja has been primarily perpetuated by literature, propaganda posters and, of course, cinema. Hollywood portrays the ninja in one of two ways: either as a heartless, cold-blooded assassin or as a bumbling, pizza-loving sewer dweller. Both stereotypes are dangerous and can lead to some confusing conversations.

THE "COLD ASSASSIN" STEREOTYPE

According to a recent survey, 87 percent of Americans believe that "all ninjas are villainous murderers with no regard for human life." This is simply not true. When you encounter a bigot who believes in this particular ninja stereotype, you will be met with fear and hatred. These bigots will not befriend you. They will not help you cross the street when you become an old, gray-haired ninja. They will not offer you a shoulder to lean on when you are tying your *jika-tabi*.

HOW TO DEAL WITH "NINJA-ASSASSIN" BIGOTS

These particular *anti-ninjites* must be dealt with subtly and carefully. The easiest and most obvious method, and the one that most newcomers to ninjahood choose, is the "assassinate" method. This method, as implied by its name, is the method of murdering to death anyone who thinks all ninjas are murderers.

Unfortunately, the elimination of anti-ninjites through assassination only perpetuates the "cold assassin" stereotype. Moreover, murder is frowned upon in the majority of the U.S. and should only be attempted if you meet an anti-ninjite on a private yacht in open international waters.

The best approach is the "re-education" method, whereby you follow a set of talking points proven to turn even the most hardened ninja-skeptic into a veritable ninjaphile.

"RE-EDUCATION" TALKING POINTS

- Admittedly, many ninjas have done things that most people would regret. But really, who hasn't accidentally taken one too many free samples, skipped paying for public transit or accidentally disemboweled a bystander?

- It's the media! The 24-hour news cycle focuses unfairly on these "bad ninjas."

- Thousands of ninjas live normal, peaceful lives, owning small dogs and driving Jettas.

- Many ninjas are humanitarians who enjoy activities like caring for old people, community gardening and scrapbooking for the poor.

- As for these "assassinations"? We ninjas didn't hear you complaining when Hitler "committed suicide," Stalin "died of natural causes" or Bin Laden "developed chronically low blood pressure."

THE "TURTLE" STEREOTYPE

The 1980s were a rough 10 years for ninjas, to say the least. Society was flooded with endless kitschy fads such as slap bracelets and parachute pants as well as inaccurate ninja movies such as *The Karate Kid* and *Teenage Mutant Ninja Turtles*. The latter movie cast ninjas in the worst light possible: as Italophile moronic reptiles with an illiterate sewer rat for a teacher. The wounds inflicted on the ninja community were so deep that hundreds of ninjas left dojos from Denver to Detroit to escape the ridicule. It would take another 20 years for the ninja population to recover, just in time for the remake of *The Karate Kid*.

CHAPTER 12

THE FAMOUS NINJA BATTLE DIET: DEVOUR THIS, NOT THAT

"Before I tried the Ninja Battle Diet, I was only able to last for three to five minutes, but now I can go long and hard for hours on end."

— Donald M., Ninja convert

A BRIEF HISTORY OF CONSUMABLES

Food. Delicious, nutritious, life-sustaining and fattening, food is as much a curse as it is a vital blessing. As we make our way into the 21st century, food has evolved into such a spectacular melding of art and science that it would please even the bastard child of Van Gogh and Galileo. The process of cultivating and distributing comestibles requires a complicated global network, an intricate system of vast, biotech-enhanced farmlands, extensive shipping routes and the most overweight humans in history.

The Ninja Food Pyramid—Sweets/Wasabi/ Fish and Poultry/Rice/Green Tea/Sake.

In today's Western world, our edible options are endless. But while foods can be inexpensive and delicious, they are more often than not unhealthy. During the course of human evolution, the tongue developed a preference for high-energy foods such as sugars and fats. This inclination befitted us during our late-caveman/early-ninja days, when hunting large animals was dangerous and our sweets came from temperamental natural high-fructose sources such as honey, fruits and berries, breast milk and certain root vegetables. But today, our meats are processed with unhealthy doses of transfat, superfluous sodium and chemical preservatives, and our sweets come from fructose imposters such as sucrose and high-fructose corn syrup. The resultant products are tasty and viscerally appealing but extremely unhealthy, and can have profoundly negative effects such as obesity, clogged arteries, tooth decay, halitosis and extreme lethargy.

To be a successful ninja, you must completely rethink your entire diet.

THE FAMOUS NINJA BATTLE DIET

On the Ninja Battle Diet, you will be limited to simple, unprocessed foods such as rice, seaweed and pine needles. You will not be permitted to have more than nine ounces of meat per week, and all

Don't be a fatty!

of your meals will be prepared without olive oil, butter or salt. As a result, your food will be about as bland as a churchgoer on Sunday.

But should you successfully follow the Ninja Battle Diet, you will find yourself filled with a constant abundance of untamable vigor. This sustained energy peak will benefit you in both battles and your social life, allowing you to fight with greater endurance, quickness and mental agility and then go home and demolish your girlfriend or mother in a heated argument.

✳ ✳ ✳

DEVOUR THIS, NOT THAT: THE NINJA BATTLE DIET'S 10 FOODS YOU SHOULD AND SHOULDN'T EAT

DEVOUR THIS

Rice: It may be whiter and more boring than the entire Republican Party, and you may have to eat more than 8,000 grains a day to quench your hunger, but rice should be a staple in every ninja's diet. High in carbohydrates but almost completely void of fats and sugars, rice provides you with high, sustained energy to keep you going strong all battle long. Rice can be boiled, steamed, sautéed with vegetables, ground into a flour to make rice milk and sake, or stretched into noodles. *Warning:* Rice lacks essential amino acids and is therefore not a complete protein. *Suitable Replacements:* Naturally grown maize, wheat and oats, and, for hipsters, Trader Joe's–brand quinoa.

NOT THAT

Prepackaged Foods: Although you will be busy balancing ninja training, your career and the fractured fragments of a social life, you must not, under any circumstance, allow yourself to eat a quick, preservative-packed prepackaged meal. These damaging MREs are laden with body-debilitating chemicals such as sodium and unpronounceable additives such as xyglonium, maglobloglobloglobin, and the ubiquitous watthefuckisthat. Avoid packaged foods at all costs, even if you find them at ninja-friendly supermarkets such as Trader Joji's or Whole Foods & Swords.

DEVOUR THIS

Legumes: Diverse, flavorful and rich in essential amino acids, legumes such as lentils, soy and mung beans provide the perfect supplement to a rice-heavy diet. Essential amino acids are, as the name implies, a necessary part of any normal human's diet. In point of fact, the human body can only produce a fraction of the amino acids that it requires for survival. You may want to enjoy your legumes with your rice, as the combination creates a subtle and delicious balance of flavors and nutrients.

NOT THAT

French Fries: The potato is a magical, unclassifiable root. Not vegetable, fruit or meat, this ugly, dirt-o-phile tuber not only helped *build* the Republic of Ireland, it also helped *destroy* it during the great Irish potato famine. You can live off the potato. Make weapons from it. Warm it up and use it to soothe your achy muscles. But whatever you do, don't fry it. Deep frying anything tends to leach out nutrients and replace them with unhealthy fats and self-doubt. The only exception is, of course, tempura.

DEVOUR THIS

Human Breast Milk (HBM): Granted, a fresh bottle of human breast milk is not as easy to get as a bottle of 2-percent straight from a cow, but it is a whole lot healthier. In addition to providing the magical mixture of carbohydrates, protein and sugars, HBM also provides an unbelievable slew of vitamins, minerals, digestive enzymes and hormones. As if the nutritional supply weren't enough, human breast milk also gives the consumer a euphoric buzz by supplying endocannabinoids, the very same neurotransmitters stimulated by marijuana. As a final added bonus, HBM significantly reduces the risk of SIDS (Sudden Infant Death Syndrome), and is therefore a must for all infant ninja trainees. *Suitable Replacements:* If you are unable to find human breast milk, certain other varieties of mammalian breast milk will provide an adequate substitute.

Elephants: Elephants, which have a similar social structure and emotional temperament to humans, produce very similar breast milk to humans. In fact, elephant milk is the only nonhuman milk that provides olichosacharides, complex sugars that stimulate advanced brain growth and adult neurogenesis.

Snow Leopards: The animal most similar to the ninja in a physical sense, the snow leopard also provides a special blend of breast milk that promotes alertness, quickness, balance, dexterity and beautiful skin patterns.

NOT THAT

Dairy Milk: Overloaded with antioxidant-leaching casein, cow's milk will eventually kill you. Aside from the health risks, dairy cows produce a thicker, blander variety of milk than their human counterparts, making for a much more boring and viscous consumption experience.

DEVOUR THIS

Wasabi: Made from the wild radishes found in horse pastures, wasabi is an integral spice that can enhance the flavors of almost any bland meal. Ground into a cream paste, wasabi is not only a delicious addition to rice, lentils, meat or fish, but because of its spicy properties, it also can give you a jolt of necessary adrenaline during a sudden battle or intimidating bar experience. *Suitable Replacements:* When eating Mexican or South American cuisine, you may want to replace wasabi with a pepper-based hot-sauce such as Crystal, Tapatio, or Trader Joji's Flamin' Anus Habenero Sauce.

NOT THAT

Garlic: Although good for the heart and a delicious addition to many a meal, garlic causes severely bad breath, and as any experienced ninja can tell you, halitosis can ruin the element of surprise and thus impede an otherwise well-planned attack or espionage mission. In general, avoid all foods that cause bad breath or smells, including hot dogs, strong cheeses, sulphurs and certain asparagus. *Try Instead:* Finely chopped sautéed pine needles provide a similar garlicky flavor boost, but without any of the associated strong, negative smells.

DEVOUR THIS

Pine Needles: Pine needles grow abundantly in nearly all regions of America, and are generally not consumed by humans or other animals. Historically, humans (and nearly all species of animals) have been unable to digest pine needles. According to biologists, we lack the necessary enzymes to break down the thick chains of starch. However, this is a fat, steaming crock of crap. By simply exercising a little self-discipline, any beginning ninja can easily master the ancient and highly useful art of pine needle digestion. The clever ninja who develops the ability to digest pine needles will have a leg up on the rest of the human race, as he will be able to find a snack on any prolonged chase, espionage mission or backpacking trip.

NOT THAT

Sugar and Corn Syrup: Avoid eating any unnecessary sugar. Again, your sweets intake should come exclusively from natural sources such as fruits, berries or breast milk. Avoid Oreo cookies, ice cream, sugar in your coffee or anything with sugar or corn syrup on its list of ingredients. *Try Instead:* Sex, cocaine and gambling activate the same neural pathways as sugar, resulting in that familiar and always desirable high.

DEVOUR THIS

Green Tea: Capable of increasing your metabolism and infusing your body with life-preserving antioxidants and a constant stream of Viagra-like sexual stimulants, green tea is one of nature's most revered superfoods. The small amount of caffeine is just enough to keep you up during a late-night assassination mission, yet low enough to prevent your *shuriken*-wielding hands from getting the shakes.

NOT THAT

Coffee: Although it provides powerful antioxidants and a short-term energy boost, coffee is a major mistake. As far as stimulants go, coffee is relatively unimpressive, as it only provides you with about 30 minutes of pure energy, generally followed by a sudden crash. Coffee can give you the leg up during short, easy bouts, but will almost always prove deadly during epic ninja battles. *Try Instead:* Green tea, bull's semen or a vitamin B–packed 36-hour energy drink.

DEVOUR THIS

Sake (The Gatorade of the East): Brewed from fermented rice water and a pinch of virgin blood, Japan's rice wine, or sake, is the intoxicant of choice for all aspiring ninjas. Low in fat and sugars yet rich in flavor, sake provides that oh-so-desired state of drunkenness followed by a surprisingly mellow hangover. Perfect for post-battle celebrations or just to ease the pressure on a first date, sake can be served hot or cold, filtered or unfiltered, with or without company and makes a perfect pairing for a variety of meals and snacks.

NOT THAT

Beer: Although this libation is a favorite in nearly every country around the world, it is intensely unsuitable for ninja consumption. Even the lightest and crappiest beers are filled with empty calories and carbohydrates that will leave you feeling bloated, lethargic and wondering who the hell you slept with last night. Take extra precaution to avoid heavy beers such as Guinness or any porter, as well as brown, red, IPA, wheat, amber, white or Belgian ale.

A QUICK NOTE ABOUT SALT WATER

As you will soon learn, much of a ninja's life is spent at sea. Ninjas and pirates have had a long, violent history, and aquatic navigation is an integral part of many ninja missions. There have been reports of several ninjas dying of thirst on seafaring missions, despite being surrounded by water. You must learn to distill salt water, as it will save your life an average of three times per year.

CHAPTER 13

ADVANCED NINJA TRAINING

PREPARING FOR ADVANCED NINJA TRAINING

Now that you've completed a few grueling weeks of beginner's ninja training, it's time to move on to honing the ultimate techniques. In this chapter you'll learn such important skills as planning a covert mission; hand-to-hand combat against multiple drunk attackers; walking across water without wetting yourself; and expert evasion tactics such as front rolls, cartwheels, standing jumps and flailing spins.

SHEDDING YOUR WESTERN TRAINING

Having completed your initial weeks of training, you're probably getting a little cocky. You're heading into these final weeks of conditioning with a pair of bowling balls in your pants and a tiger in your heart. Take it easy, Kimosabe, you're not there yet. You may know how to rip an American cartwheel, bust an Oregonian somersault, run a marathon in a New York minute, or jump a Denver mile, but your American athleticism is no match for the ninja ways you are about to learn.

THE FOUNDATIONS OF ADVANCED NINJA TRAINING

Strength: During your initial transitional phase, you began to experiment with beginning strength-training exercises. Now it's time to put those newly grown muscles to the test. As a ninja, being Popeye-strong is not good enough; instead, you must posses the strength of an elephant bull on steroids.

Speed: As you've probably already guessed, ninjas have cheetahlike speed that comes from an intense amount of long-distance running and hard wind sprints. A recent ninja census determined that ninjas run an average of 6,570 miles per year (18 miles per day).

Flexibility: As a ninja, a pulled muscle or torn ligament will surely mean your life. Besides survival, extreme dexterity will help the aspiring ninja succeed in all sorts of situations, such as kicking really tall enemies in the face, twisting into really tight hiding places and inventing unique, impressive love-making maneuvers.

Silence: The start of your ninja training was all about perfecting the little things that would "ninjaize" you. Learning the initial moves has been about training muscle memory. Now it's time to add the element of silence. After all, the ninja's greatest asset is his ability to do awesome things without making a sound.

Vocabulary: A good Japanese vocabulary is essential to completing your training. Make sure you know the following phrases by heart:

Aitsu wa chimamire data: He was covered in blood.

Nigero: Run away!

Sumata: Dry humping

Ganguro: Super-tan

Jikan wakarimasuka?: Do you have the time?

✳ ✳ ✳

ADVANCED NINJA MOVEMENTS

ADVANCED WALKING

To walk quietly, follow the following four points.

1. Swing your legs out wide with each step.

2. Land first on your outside back heel. (A full-footed landing is noisy.)

3. Roll the outside edge of your foot forward.

4. Spring forward from you inside toe.

ADVANCED *NIPPON* FRONT ROLL

The classic ninja somersault is the building block of most ninja moves. The ninja rolls, or *nippon*, is used as the primary means of escaping a rear-launched attack, and is the primary technique in moving toward an enemy quickly and quietly while reducing your vulnerable attack areas.

To execute a proper ninja front roll, keep to the following instructional diagram.

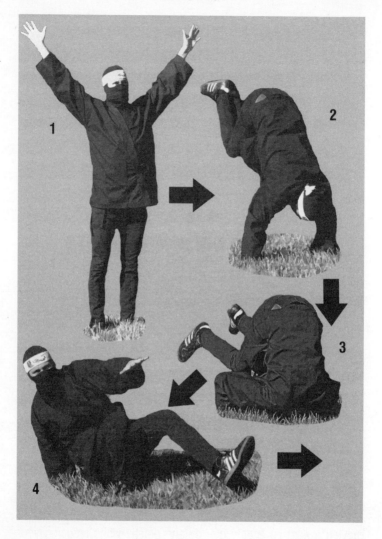

1. Push off your feet with your hands outstretched.
2. Place both hands firmly on the ground.
3. Tuck your head into your chest, rounding your spine.
4. Roll over your back, using your speed to launch up and out of the roll.
5. Tack on a sword-attack-straight-legged-kick combo to debilitate awestruck foes.

SHIKOKU JUMP

From early childhood, most Americans are taught a basic way to spring off the ground using their leg muscles. This upward movement, or "jump," is more often than not accompanied by a noticeably audible landing, often termed an "American return"; the noisiness of the American return is due to a complex chain reaction upon touchdown. First, the jumper's feet hit the surface flat, producing a sudden torso constriction, which causes the jumper to expunge a lungful of air and finally results in one of three noisy results: (a) loud exhale, (b) guttural grunt or (c) involuntary defecation.

The advanced *shikoku* jump takes the "(wh-)ump" out of "jump":

1. Pump one fist into the air, keeping the other one at your side for counterbalance. (This will ensure maximum elevation.)

2. Kick one foot backward, grabbing your big toe with your non-elevated hand.

3. Land on the balls of your feet.

4. When you feel contact, tuck your rectum toward your heels. This will ensure that your torso does not constrict.

5. Spread arms out wide and point your fingers, to ensure lateral balance.

HIGH-ALTITUDE *NUKA* FLOP

As a ninja, you will naturally spend a large portion of your day jumping, repelling or diving off of tall objects. Whether you're launching from a small hiding tree, car roof, telephone pole, giant sequoia or plane, you must perfect the art of the *nuka* flop to avoid the pain of landing.

Instead of hitting the ground feet-first and crumpling into a ball of broken bones and punctured organs, try this simple ninja technique to perfectly disperse the force of landing:

1. Again, you must pump one fist into the air, keeping the other one at your side for counterbalance.
2. Point your toes toward the ground so you land on the balls of your feet.
3. Bend your knees slightly and let your hip point toward your raised arm.
4. Allow your body to fall to the side of your raised arm with your head leaning away from the direction of the fall.
5. Let your body roll over the ground toward your extended hand, naturally rocking into a sick one-armed handstand.

HOIRU SUBARASHII (AWESOME WHEEL)

A thief's fully loaded shotgun is aimed point-blank at your heaving sternum. You have one second to evade a spray of deadly lead. What do you do? Common sense tells you to drop and play dead so he won't bother you; but your ninja training should tell you to cartwheel the shit out of there. Capable of taking you up to 10 feet laterally in a flash, the *hoiru subarashii* is one of the most important defensive moves in a ninja's arsenal. Beautiful to behold, a properly executed ninja cartwheel can be extraordinarily impressive—and may even get you laid.

The following is a properly executed *hoiru subarashii*:

1. Launch to one side with your arms and legs together, bending your torso toward the ground.

2. Place your inside hand on the ground, flinging a ninja star with your free hand.

3. As your feet reach their penultimate position, unleash a dazzling flurry of upside-down kicks at your opponent.

4. Land your cartwheel in an intimidating stance like Shitting Bull, Licking Dog or Engorged Daffodil.

✳ ✳ ✳

ADVANCED CLIMBING TECHNIQUES AND LOCATIONS

Climbing is one of the most important skills in your proverbial ninja fanny pack. Good climbing skills can help you evade an assailant during an attack or simply get you to a strategic espionage perch. Knowing how to scale and descend from the following locations is a must for all ninjas.

Utility Poles: Telephone polls are easy to climb and make excellent espionage perches. Once there, you can easily steal cable or attach a phone line for a static-free call. When climbing a utility poll, it is vital that you dress as a cable worker or telephone utility employee, otherwise a neighbor may call the cops or shoot you. *Helpful Hint:* When climbing a utility poll for purposes of espionage, make sure your chosen perch has a view of your spy target.

Apartment Buildings: While on assassination missions, beginning ninjas often make the mistake of entering a target's domicile through the main entry. However, because most targets will have at least some knowledge that an attack may be imminent, they may be watchful of their front door. Instead of making this beginner's entrance, climb the side of your target's building and enter through the window. This will ensure a stealth entry, but it will also give you ample opportunity to spray-paint your ninja name on the building façade, which is a great way to advertise your services.

Redwood Trees: Ninjas have a long and sordid history with redwood trees. They've used them in poems, analogies and metonyms. They've used their wood to fashion *yumi* bows and finely polished serving dishes. But most of all, since their early forays in America's Pacific wilderness, ninjas have regarded these mammoths of the cypress family as the world's most luxurious hiding locales. Difficult to ascend initially due to their branchless trunks, the upper limbs afford up to 400 feet of covert canopy along with a diverse ecosystem ninjas can thrive in for months.

To climb a redwood, you must use *shuku* ("tiger claws"), clever little things that go on your feet and hands and have spikes you can drive into the redwood bark. Purchase your *shuku* from your local ninja shop or Amazon.com. If you don't want to use these handy gloves due to environmental concerns, you can nakedly "free climb" the redwood. To do so, "hug" the trunk with your arms and legs, pressing into it with the insides of your elbows and inner thighs. Dig into the bark with your toenails, fingernails and teeth.

The Social Ladder: Ninjas don't just use their *ninjutsu* skills to physically climb; they also use their ninjaness to become more popular. Climbing the social ladder the ninja way is best achieved through the ancient ninja technique of "rung skipping," and should only be attempted by expert ninjas. This masterful skill entails quickly dismissing new friends for those at least twice as rich and powerful.

RAPPELLING

Ninjutsu outlines several rappelling techniques that can aid a quick and stealthy escape or help you dangle just below a victim's line of sight.

Repelling from Burning Buildings: Early in your ninja career, you will probably accidentally burn down several buildings. Learning how to quickly rappel down the façade of a burning building will save you from a very overcooked destiny. The trick to a quick descent is to utilize gravity instead of fighting against it. Use your legs to push away from the building. Then let gravity to its work. Remember to hold the rope loosely, letting it slide through you fingers like sand or a gentle breeze. *Helpful Hint:* When rappelling, make sure to remove any capes or wings you may be wearing, as these can hinder a stealthy descent.

Dangling: The art of dangling can be helpful during espionage missions and on dates. *For Espionage Missions*: Dangling just beneath a target's window, you will be able to hear their words and movements without sacrificing your anonymity. *For Dates:* Girls go crazy for nice views. Instead of going to Lover's Point or some expensive rotating restaurant, try sharing a picnic while suspended from the side of a tall building. We guarantee your date will appreciate the gesture of originality.

✳ ✳ ✳

ADVANCED MARITIME-FIGHTING TECHNIQUES

When the U.S. Navy was developing their famed Slippery Eel After Lunch (SEAL) program, they turned to the highly talented ninjas of the Pacific Ocean for guidance. Over hundreds of years, the notorious Pacific Rim Aquatically Weaponized Ninjas (PRAWN) had turned their aquatic domain into a veritable arsenal of highly trained marine mammals, weapons crafted from the sea's natural defenses and a whole host of throwing fish.

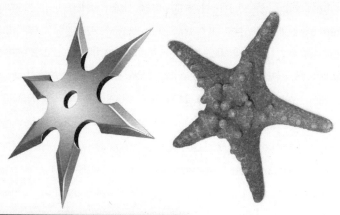

Terrestrial and aqueous versions of the ninja-star

Even if you live a thousand miles from the nearest beach, you should still develop the necessary skills for fighting in a saltwater environment. Harnessing the immense power of the sea is one of the ninja's foremost weapons.

"PACK FISH" AND DOMESTICATED SEA LIFE

The advent of maritime radar, swift boats and binoculars has rendered the rowboat and swimming arms poor choices for highly trained ninjas. Today, most advanced ninjas prefer utilizing the ocean's naturally intelligent organisms for travel and defense. The ocean is chock-full of "horses of the sea," each with its unique benefits and pitfalls.

Dolphins: In the ocean or at SeaWorld, dolphins are a ninja's best friends. With their keen intellects, excellent communication skills, sleeplessness and fast but silent underwater speed, dolphins are excellent riding pets for pirate chases or other offshore activities.

Dolphins are playful and very sexual, though, so it is important to give them a play break every several hours, either by letting them surf waves, torment turtles, molest seagulls, or flirt with other dolphins. You may also want to learn to speak dolphin, an advanced language involving clicks, whistles, and the hard-to-master burst-pulses. Also, keep in mind that dolphins are giant wussies, as they are the only altruistic nonhuman species. This means that if you try to drown a target, the dolphin may carry him up to the surface.

Whales: Whales are larger, smellier and slightly less ninja-friendly than dolphins, but they do offer luxury, comfort and speed that their smaller cetacean cousins just can't match. Keep in mind that, like dolphins, these Cadillacs of the sea are slaves to their appetites and will get distracted by patches of high-energy krill.

Sea Turtles: In the ninja movie *Finding Nemo*, the main characters are displayed riding tortoises at great speeds *and enjoying it*. This is pure fiction. Turtles in water make mediocre riding pets at best; even though they can swim at decent speeds (20 to 30 mph) and for up to 40 hours in succession, their rough, segmented shells make for uncomfortable riding surfaces with little room for storage.

OCEAN WEAPONS

The sea is home to millions of natural weapons, so feel free to leave your ninja satchel at home when hitting the beach.

***Ryuboku Bo* (Driftwood Staffs):** Strong, abundant and reeking of rotting sea life, *ryuboku bo* make for brutal weapons as well as excellent flotation devices when you get tired. The staffs are also ideal for seaside bonfires when dried.

Shark Teeth: Sharp and calcium-hard, shark teeth have been used for millennia by Pacific natives to add an extra bite to brutal war clubs and mallets. The serrated teeth can also be fastened to the end of your *ryuboku bo* to form a top-notch spear.

Spearfish (Marlin): The name pretty much says it all. While spearfish can be trained as natural missiles to target scuba divers and even weekend fishermen, at 1,500 pounds, they are far too heavy to be easily wielded by hand.

Starfish (Sea Stars): As their name suggests, starfish are the ocean's "natural ninja star." While sea stars are neither as aerodynamic (nor aquadynamic, for that matter) nor sharp as *shuriken*, they can still leave a nice welt on an opponent's skin if thrown with enough velocity and torque.

Kelp: About the same shape, length, weight and flexibility as a ninja rope, a whipped kelp bulb will sting several times worse than a locker-room towel slap, and a well-aimed kelp whip can even be deadly, wrapping around an opponent's neck or torso and squeezing the life out him.

Poisonous Critters: Electric eels, box jellyfish, lionfish and water snakes can be thrown at an opponent, often inducing death or, at the very least, an aquarium-style thrill.

Sea Anemones: Used in the ocean, where most blinding powders end up as damp clumps, sharp sea anemones can be thrown directly at an opponent's face, where they will stick, rendering your opponent temporarily blind.

The *Ika* Squeeze: In the ocean, where smoke bombs and evasion powders are useless, the *ika* (squid) is the tool of choice. A well-squeezed squid will scream, creating an auditory distraction, and excrete a cloud of thick black squid ink, providing enough cover for you to initiate an assault or make your escape. As an added bonus, you can use leftover squid ink to leave messages for trailing ninja cohorts or nearby sexy snorkelers.

✹ ✹ ✹
KAYAKUJUTSUS
(THE ART OF PYROTECHNICS)

Ninjas are experts with flames, fires, smoke, firecrackers, barbecues and all sorts of flame-related elements. In the early days of ninjaness, ninjas would mainly use exploding powders for distraction, but when the gun was brought to Japan, some dojos began perfecting the art of firing guns, canons, launchers and even tactical nuclear weaponry. In a landmark reversal, the GNC (Global Ninja Coalition) banned all use of firearms and bombs in 1979. But ninjas remain masters of the flame.

Building a Fire: The simplest and most ancient utility of pyrotechnics is the Art of Building a Fire, which will help keep you warm, provide enough concentrated heat to cook meats that might otherwise contain dangerous bacteria, and can be used to burn down a plethora of things. There are several techniques for fire-building, including the old-fashioned lightning bolt harness, the ubiquitous match or lighter technique or the slightly more frustrating flint strike, refracted lens and hot potato methods.

The Ninja Fire-Starting Method: Ninjas, of course, practice none of the above mainstream fire-starting methods. Instead, they utilize the ancient technique of "pyro-optico-burnia." Similar to the refracted lens method, pyro-optico-burnia requires you to kill and enucleate an animal or human and then use his detached eyeball as a lens to magnify the sun's heat onto a tinder nest. If you don't know what a tinder nest is, you may want to reconsider your decision to go ninja.

Smoke-Free Fires: In the West, there are four elements: earth, air, fire and water. In the East there are five: earth, air, fire, water and energy. Ninjas, on the other hand recognize only one: the element

of surprise. As such, a blue plume of wispy smoke wafting above the tree line may seem innocuous, but it can ruin the ninja's one true element and potentially cost the s'more-indulging ninja their mission or even their life. Thus, mastering the tricky art of the smokeless fire is a necessity for all ninja students:

1. Create an open "log-cabin stack" of small dry logs, allowing for as much oxygen as possible to enter the burn zone. Do not use any live or green wood or leaves.

2. Continuously feed the fire with small dry twigs. Smoke is created when the surface area of the logs burns inconsistently. By adding the quick-burning twigs, the fire should burn more evenly, reducing the smoke to almost invisible levels.

3. When roasting marshmallows, take extreme caution not to lose any of the tasty puffs in the fire, as they are very prone to producing excessive smoke.

4. Do not indulge in tobacco, marijuana or any type of Scandinavian smoked fish during this process.

CHAPTER 14

CONVERSATIONAL JAPANESE

The following is a typical conversation you might have while trying to make friends as a ninja. The text has been provided in both phonetic Japanese and English to make learning easier.

Introduce yourself:

Ore wa Davu te iunda.

Hi, my name is Dave.

Get blown off:

Saitei da omae, Davu.

You suck, Dave.

Reply politely. It is the way of the ninja.

Suimasen?

I beg your pardon?

This jackass is having none of your common courtesy:

Kusokurae otaku.

Eat shit, nerd.

This fool has just disrespected a budding ninja? Keep it calm. Stretch your neck muscles and simply inform him:

Machigatte iru ninja no ani to issho ni anata ga seikō.

You fuck with the wrong ninja, bro.

Follow that up with something awesome. It will impress and intimidate:

Watashi wa doragon no honoo no yōna bōru o gozen!

I am the dragon's fiery balls!

Should your opponent whip out a savage *ninja-to* of his own, chances are, you're about to get your bleed on. At this point listen for:

Dono yō ni shinu koto o go kibōdesu ka?

How would you prefer to die?

At which moment you should unleash your best Dead Possum Stance and declare:

Yoroshiku onegai amigo shimasu!

My mistake, amigo. Let's be friends!

Part Three:
Living the Ninja Life

CHAPTER 15

REACHING NINJA MATURITY

RE-ASSIMILATING TO THE AMERICAN NINJA LIFESTYLE

Assimilation is arguably the most important part of being a modern ninja. Chances are that you decided to go ninja not because you wanted to escape your world, but because you wanted to become a more lofty part of it. Today, re-assimilation into American society is not only accepted but encouraged.

One of the greatest powers of the ninja is the ability to thrive in any situation. Because impersonation is such a vital aspect of espionage, ninja masters have always encouraged their students to adapt to new environments and keep up with the tides of cultural change.

In historic Japan, adapting meant being a social chameleon—being versed in cultural practices and personalities of people from every city, town and stratum. When ninjas began to live abroad during the Dark Ages, assimilation became even more important. In countries with lenient immigration policies, ninjas were free to keep their cultural heritage, but more often than not, they were forced to fully adapt to the ways of their new homeland. Of course, ninjas—being ninjas—transformed these new social constructs into subtle versions of their own.

Today, the practice of "partial assimilation" is still considered a must. The American Ninja Institute, which provides resources and guidelines for American and foreign ninjas living in the U.S., encourages practitioners to "espouse modern American philosophies, aesthetics and lifestyle choices, to a limited extent, so that you may fit in without losing too much of your ninja identity." In this chapter, we will outline various contemporary American social constructs and show you how to twist them so they are distinctly ninja.

✳ ✳ ✳

PICKING A NINJA PET

As an American, it's important to have a pet or two, but as a ninja, it's vital to distinguish yourself from your ordinary canine- and feline-loving friends. Choosing an animal to dwell inside your home reflects directly on your character. These days, most ninjas forgo the one or two pet norm and opt instead for a veritable menagerie, one consisting of both wild beasts and productive creatures. When developing your menagerie, consider how the size of your home and sensitivity of your nose may affect your ability to care for a particular pet.

Adorable teacup tigers make excellent pets for the apartment-dwelling ninja.

Silkworms: Practical, small and easy to keep, these industrious caterpillars are an excellent choice for the studio-apartment-dwelling ninja. As a bonus, each silkworm produces about 2,000 feet of raw silk.

Kōji: Combine a love of science and a ninja pressed for spare time and space, and a cozy colony of *kōji* mold might be just the ticket. An essential ingredient in producing sake, this fast-growing mold resembles a microscopic collection of adorable gerbils.

NINJA PET ESSENTIALS: THE *TANUKI*

No animal is more essential to a ninja's menagerie than the mischievous *tanuki*. Native to Japan and known in America as "the

raccoon dog," these incredible creatures have rightly earned their reputation as "Japan's Original Ninja" by being masters of disguise and mind control. The magical powers of these highly evolved furballs include:

Shapeshifting: Young *tanuki* can take on the shapes of natural brown things, such as tree boughs, bamboo rods or fecal droppings, while more mature *tanuki* can assume the appearance of man-made items such as metallic tea kettles or wads of cash.

Disproportionally Humongous Testicles: While these at first may seem like a burden, a *tanuki* can sling his sac over his shoulder and use it as a backpack; the more rhythmic ones can provide hours of entertainment by using his balls as drums. Mature *tanuki* can achieve great speeds and bounce to incredible heights by using their giant testicles like a natural bouncy ball.

Sake Drinking: When lonely, would you rather cuddle with a dog or get drunk with a talking raccoon-dog? *Tanuki* make excellent drinking companions, but be careful around billiard and card tables, as *tanuki* are known to be hustlers when intoxicated.

Petty Thievery: *Tanuki* are mischievous and love to steal anything from an old woman's purse to an ancient scroll to a steaming bowl of ramen.

Don't expect your friends to believe you when you tell them your furry companion has magical powers. For thousands of years, *tanuki* have never revealed their mythical powers to a non-ninja.

Japanese Serows: Furry, gray and downright adorable, the Japanese serow is the boxy, even-tempered "miniature schnauzer of the goat-antelope family." The cuddly 260-pound creatures enjoy rugged hikes, eating leaves and luxuriating on precarious rock ledges in the afternoon. Not ideal for ninjas with small children, but the perfect pet if you've got a large, mountainous backyard.

Indochinese Tiger: For ninjas who've raised temperamental house cats in the past, the rare Indochinese tiger is a natural choice. While many animal experts state that these lethal predatory felines make dangerous pets, the only real drawback to the tiger is how much it enjoys snuggling.

❉ ❉ ❉

PACK ANIMALS: HORSES, ELEPHANTS, CAMELS, POLAR BEARS AND DOLPHINS

Back when ninja operations were confined to the islands of Japan, ninjas stuck with easily tamed horses. Today, however, ninjas must adapt to the wide diversity of terrains found around the world. Owning a variety of pack animals and choosing the appropriate species for each mission are essential components to your mobility on the job. For example, choose elephants for dense jungle missions or African safaris. Camels are ideal for desert travel. Polar bears are the choice of snowbound ninjas, and the friendly dolphin is an excellent way to navigate coastal waters.

Ninja Boarding Stables: Chances are your home is not large enough to fit every pack animal you will need for your missions and battles. As an alternative, you may want to think of housing your stock at your local ninja boarding stable. Found in most major metropolitan areas, ninja boarding stables not only provide housing for your pack animals, but their trained technicians will also feed, walk, groom and play with your pets daily to ensure they have a long and healthy life.

ADVANCED BAREBACK RIDING TECHNIQUES

Owning a variety of riding pets is only half the battle; in addition, you must not only know which animal is best suited for a particular mission, but you must also have the ability to ride and control each riding pet. To be a successful ninja, you must work on a variety of advanced riding techniques so you are prepared for any animal you encounter.

Know Your Pet: The first step to riding a pet is to gain its trust. As most ninja pets are temperamental, finicky and often violent, it is essential that you get to know all your pets on both a physical and a mental level. Give each of your pets names, learn their personalities and figure out exactly how they like to be touched.

Location: The most important aspect of riding is to know your terrain—and to choose the right steed for each particular area. A ninja working in Manhattan, for example, will have little use for an elephant, but by riding a well-trained California condor you can soar well-above New York's skyscrapers. Another New York option is the giant kangaroo, which can easily hop over cars and pedestrians and into whose pouch you can easily slip.

Navigation Communication: You must learn to communicate silently with your pet, so that it will turn, accelerate, decelerate and stop at your behest. Riding pets can be tricky; some prefer receiving instructions in soft, soothing voices, while others prefer to be roughly cajoled.

Sitting: Not every riding pet's back is the same, and many are quite uncomfortable to sit on. For longer journeys, you may want to fashion a saddle or seat to suit your chosen animal.

Bring Food: Although it may seem obvious, you must bring enough sustenance to slake your thirst and quench your hunger for the duration of the journey. Many ninjas have underpacked and been forced to eat their steeds.

CHAPTER 16

CHOOSING YOUR NINJA CLAN

For you, the budding ninja, the moment you choose a clan is the most important moment of your life. Not only will it determine your future career path, but it will also dictate what type of ninjas you will be around for the rest of your life, and therefore what type of ninja you yourself will become. In the United States, the five overarching *ryu* (clans or "ninja unions") comprise almost 60 percent of America's active ninjas. If you can get into one of these clans, you're almost guaranteed work for life as long as you pay your dues.

Keep in mind, however, that getting into a ninja clan, especially one of the "Big Five," is extremely stressful. Each clan has rigorous application standards, including background checks, dangerous skills tests and a written essay. Only the top 30 percent of ninjas are accepted into clans, so when applying, be realistic about your chances.

THE APPLICATION PROCESS

All clans require a lengthy interview in which you will demonstrate your arsenal of ninja moves, from swordplay and *shuriken* accuracy to kicks, punches, throws and cartwheels. In addition, the clans will review your scores on the standardized American Ninjutsu Aptitude Litmus Exam that every ninja takes upon earning their mask.

AMERICAN NINJUTSU APTITUDE LITMUS EXAM

The ANAL Exam will be the most rigorous test you've ever had to take. Three hours of multiple-choice questions test your knowledge of five subjects: ninja history, pressure points, combat strategy, complex analogies and intermediate algebra.

A brief reading comprehension section (in Japanese) is followed by an essay asking you to comprehensively plan a ninja mission using only two details—place and time. This essay is perhaps the most important part of the ANAL exam, as it is used to determine both your psychological profile and your ability to think critically about a given task

Some of the more prestigious clans will also want to hold an interview. Expect these face-to-fist meetings to be extremely painful and violent, as most include simulated battles against multiple interviewers.

✳ ✳ ✳

THE BIG FIVE

Just like labor unions in the U.S., ninja employment is dominated by extremely powerful organizations. The five most prestigious clans are:

HANZŌ CLAN

The Hanzō is America's oldest ninja organization as well as its most revered. Started in 1920 by the descendants of famed ninja/funnyman Hattori Hanzō, the *ryu* has maintained a deep focus on the traditional ninja arts (culinary, acting and martial) since its inception. During the 1930s, the clan helped shape America's understanding of the ninja by producing such celebrated films as *A Ninja at the Opera* (1935), *Gone with the Shuriken* (1939) and the children's classic *The Wizard of Osaka* (1939). Today, this respected and honored *ryu* draws the best ninja creative talent from across the globe.

Membership in Hanzō is by invitation only, so you need not apply. The organization keeps a close eye on the up-and-coming ninja population and picks between 300 and 1,000 applicants annually.

Head Office Location(s): Los Angeles, California;
New York City, New York.

Members: 62,000 (2010 estimate)

Key Ninjas: Hattori "Chucky" Hanzō IX, *Jonin*
            Frank Momochi, *Head Chunin*

Founded: 1920

Website: www.hanzo-clan.org

CLAN DRAGON

The Cooperative Labor of American Ninjas is America's second oldest ninja clan and arguably the most ruthless of the Big Five. Dragonites dominate the assassination and espionage market due to strong connections with the CIA, NSA and various branches of organized crime. If you're looking for a thrill and some lucrative blood work, definitely take a shot at the Dragons.

But be warned—the Dragons' entrance exam is harrowing. Applicants are required to walk from Trenton, New Jersey, to Akron, Ohio, picking a fight with every person they pass. Those who arrive in Akron bruise-free move on to round two.

Head Office Location: Jersey City, New Jersey.

Members: 39,200 (2008 estimate)

Key Ninjas: Anthony DiMarsala, *Jonin*

Ed Hoover, *Head Chunin*

Founded: 1955

Website: www.clanofthedragon.org

STAB-ING CLAN

Society of Tax Accountants, Bankers and International Ninja Grocers is America's enormous tier-three ninja clan. In 1970, STAB (Society of Tax Accountants and Bankers) joined with ING (International Ninja Grocers) to form the country's largest and most encompassing *ryu*. Boasting over 80,000 members, STAB-ING is a great backup *ryu* for decently skilled ninjas shooting for a top organization.

Tip: It helps if you have a good background in mathematics, a high score on the ANAL Exam algebra section and a degree in accounting or statistics.

Head Office Location: Richmond, Virginia

Members: 81,000 (2010 estimate)

Key Ninjas: Barry Braunwald CPA, *Jonin*

Tracy Shawland, *Head Chunin*

Ralph Ralphs, *Head Chunin*

Founded: 1970 (STAB, 1962; ING, 1965)

Website: www.stab-ing.org

BALLS CLAN

Bicoastal American League of Laboring Shinobi is the last U.S. *ryu* we suggest trying out for. BALLS is a no-frills ninja union that offers consistent but rather unimpressive job opportunities. For your first year at BALLS, you should expect nothing more romantic than "small pet assassination" jobs—taking out the poodles, tabbies and hamsters of clients' ex-lovers and coworkers.

Be Careful: In the late 1990s, BALLS was wracked with scandal after it was discovered that many of the jobs being offered to ninjas were a part of a "Ninja Ponzi Scheme" in which members were hired to kill rival members for the *ryu*-purchased life insurance payout.

Head Office Location: Washington, D.C.

Members: 28,000

Key Ninjas: Lt. Col. Yoshi Sacamoto, *Jonin*

Bill Dangles, *Head Chunin*

Founded: 1976

Website: www.ninjaballs.org

PFNIS CLAN

Founded in 1986, the **Professional Federation of Ninja Industry and Sundries** is the *ryu* to avoid if possible. The youngest, most Canadian and least organized of the Big Five, PFNIS is an uneven mix of eager ninja startups, wannabes and washouts.

In general, PFNIS-organized gigs are hugely disappointing and most members only take the jobs if they are hard up for work. Typical employment offered by the clan includes tiger walkers, rice paper factory workers and steel miners.

Head Office Location: Toronto, Canada

Members: 9,000

Key Ninjas: Chaz Fixins, *Jonin*

             Tess Tickles, *Head Chunin*

Founded: 1986

Website: www.pfnis.org

✳ ✳ ✳

LOCAL "COMMUNITY RYUS"

If you lack the skills to get into one of the Big Five American clans, do not grab your *ninja-to* and commit *seppuku:* There's nothing embarrassing about joining a local community *ryu*, of which there are several in nearly every major metropolitan area in the Lower 48. These community clans have much more lenient admission standards, but offer lower-paying work.

Being a community ninja does not necessarily mean an impoverished life. The Big Five are always keeping a close watch on the top ninjas at most community clans, and it is not unusual for a community ninja to transfer after two or three years. In fact, some of Americas most famous and successful ninjas, including Pritchard Donahue the Elder, Cletus Steel Heart and He Who is Gary, began their careers as community ninjas.

Use your time in your community clan as a launchpad to bigger and better things. Maintain a positive attitude, petition for the most challenging work and maintain a close relationship with your clan's *jonin* and *chunin*, as they are most likely to be in communication with recruiters from the Big Five.

✳ ✳ ✳

NAVIGATING YOUR CLAN'S HIERARCHY

The complex clan structure you will encounter is sure to confuse you for the first couple of months. Here is the basic crib sheet to help you navigate the potentially embarrassing start:

Jonin: Each _ryu_ is structured much like a modern corporation or military group. At the top of the ninja pyramid is the _jonin_—the ultimate ninja. The _jonin_, usually the resident white-bearded elder, has passed all nine levels of _Ninjutsu_ Personal Development, and is a veritable top-degree ninja. The _jonin_ knows the ways of the world. Through an immense global network of field agents, he has intimate insider information about important people in every corner of the world. It takes no fewer than 85 years for a ninja to become a _jonin._

Chunin: Below the _jonin_ are the _chunin_. _Chunin_ are akin to the rank of colonels, and each _ryu_ promotes a few ninjas to the rank. _Chunin_ are usually advanced-degree ninjas who have proven their loyalty to their clan through the most trying of circumstances, and have shown superior combat skills.

Genin: _Chunin_ hand out the _jonin_'s orders to field agents known as _genin_; these underlings are the ones who execute specific assignments such as espionage, theft, sabotage, reconnaissance, assassination and kitchen detail. To clarify things, this is _you_. In order to protect the identity of members of the _ryu_, most _genin_ never know the true identity of their _jonin_. Often, multiple _genin_ will be given assignments related to the same mission (e.g., one will be sent out for reconnaissance, another for sabotage) without knowing each other's involvement.

CHAPTER 17

CHOOSING A NINJA NAME

Sara. Kelly. Sam. Keith. Traditional American names inspire neither fear nor confidence in much of anything. One of the first things you must do once you decide to go ninja is to choose an appropriate, awe-inspiring ninja name.

In the 20th century, most American ninjas chose to adopt Japanese names in order to escape from the stigma of being considered a "ninja eccentric." Today, however, a huge amount of progress has been made toward acceptance of American ninjas and ninjaism. As a result, American-sounding names comprised of English language words are now not only acceptable, but internationally respected.

TRADITIONAL NINJA NAMES

Hattori	Yamaguchi	Fuma
Kumawakamarumochi	Yagyu	Ryu
Ken	Hitachi-Hibachi	Toshiba
	Splinter	

CHOOSING A NAME

Rule #1—Pronouncability: The first rule of today's modern ninja naming is be able to pronounce your chosen name. Remember, your ninja name need not be Japanese, or even Japanese-sounding. It does not need to be romantic, foreign or ridiculously fancy. Furthermore, it should probably be in English, or at least something that is easy to pronounce. A good friend of the authors named himself Ninja Jesus Perro Roberto Ignacio de Jesus de Dia de Los Muertos. Needless to say, shortly after his naming ceremony, Jesus killed himself by putting his foot in his mouth. Not only was the name not catchy and far too long, but since he couldn't roll his *r*'s, he couldn't pronounce his own name with the required gusto. Shame.

COMMON MODERN NINJA NAMES

Crouching Spider Tooth	Virgin Martini de Sangre
Steve	El Elegante
Death on a Stick	The Black Robe
Multiple Cartwheels	Furious Fists of Rage

Rule #2—Focus on your Ninja Strength: When choosing your name, you will want to focus on your ninja skills. Think about your last week or two of training. Are there any areas of *ninjutsu* you've really excelled at? Somersaults, perhaps? Or maybe cartwheels? Either way, choosing your ninja strength is the first key to choosing a truly excellent ninja name.

Choosing a inappropriate name can be a lethal mistake: In 1994, a brash ANC named himself "Master of the Rainbow Sword," despite only receiving a score of seven on the sword wielding portion of the ANAL Exam. At a ninja convention in Brussels, Belgium later that year he was challenged by Ken of the Rusted Sword to a sword-off. Thousands of ninjas watched as Ken sliced Rainbow to brightly colored shreds. Rainbow died weeks later of rust-related tetanus.

Lesson: Do not choose your ninja name based on a weakness or include the word *rainbow*.

Rule #3—Choose Strong Adjectives: Traditionally, most ninja converts chose their name by combining an adjective with a noun or the present participle form of a ninja action verb. However, many early American Ninja Converts chose obvious, standard adjectives such as cool, badass or scary, becoming Cool Ninja, Badass Swordsman or Scary Dude. Names constructed with weak, overused adjectives make weak, overused ninjas.

In the late 00s, author Keith successfully used Choosing a Ninja Name Rules #1 and #2 by giving himself a pronounceable name based on his ninja strength: Testiculus Delight. This name, needless to say, was weak, and coauthor Sam made endless fun of Keith, until Keith eventually took on a more subtle and ominous name: Glorious Manparts. Which name do you think is scarier?

Trite, English-language adjectives are passé, a thing of America's red, white and blue past. Choosing a modern American ninja name requires an excellent vocabulary, or at least a toilet-side consultation with a top-notch thesaurus.

Rule #4—Use Creative Grammatical Structure: These days, few ninjas use the once-standard "adjective + present-participle" ninja-name construction. Instead, most experiment with different grammatical structures, such as "adjective + proper noun," "adjective + adjective" or even "pronoun + preposition + article + adjective." The grammatical structures are endless. Instead of Glorious Manparts, Keith could have further improved his name with a simple grammatical transformation: Glorious Manparts Keith, Glorious Dangerous Manparts or Keith of the Glorious Manparts.

GOING FROM PANSY TO AWESOME IN ONE SIMPLE STEP

The following ninjas started their careers with pretty awful names. After taking the Ninja Naming Seminar at Ortfield Community College Extension, these lowly ninjas turned into the famed warriors you've surely read about. Take a look at the dramatic transformation.

Dave the Speedwalker → Dave of a Quick Death

Sam the Secret Spy → Samsonite with the Large Tiger Balls

Wally Whiteman Dancing → William the Breath

Smart Ninja McGee → Brainbrain McGee

Ninja Who Wears the Black Outfit → Opaque Marauder the Late-Night Ninja of Death

Dragon Harold → Large Lizard Larry

Lil' Patrick → Patrick Large of Spirit

Donald the Bringer of Death and Flowers → Don the Death Bringer

Bad Guy the Ninja → Captain Evil

CHAPTER 18

THE NINJA GRADUATION

You've trained for grueling weeks, learned the secrets of the world's most ancient art form (*ninjutsu*), found a clan willing to sponsor you and chosen an amazing ninja name. Now it's time for you to take that last final step toward formally certified ninjahood: ninja graduation.

Besides the fact that only half of the ninjadates (ninja-candidates) survive the ritual, ninja graduation is a fairly standard graduation ceremony.

But be forewarned: Unlike your high school or college commencement, your ninja graduation is more of a trial, a final exam if you will, than a reason to drunkenly accept your diploma. It is your final test. And it will be dangerous.

The head elders will assign you several graduation assassins who will weed out the weakest ninjadates as they await their rite.

Before the head elders confer the ninja degrees, you will be pitted against other ninjadates in a series of death battles.

The key to your ninja graduation: Be prepared and know what to expect.

Location: The ceremony will be held at a location chosen by your clan leader(s). If your clan has access to a convenient facility, such as a dojo, large mansion or stadium, the ceremony will probably be held there. Some clans rent out facilities for their ceremonies, such as high-school gymnasiums, discotheques or community halls. More impoverished clans hold their ceremonies at public places such as local parks, alleys or pizza parlors.

Procession: Like most graduation ceremonies, ninja commencement includes a procession in which the ninjadates, accompanied by the head elders, walk from one place to another. Points are awarded to each ninjadate for incorporating acrobatics, style and graceful defenses into their walk. Plan on executing a few cartwheels, somersaults and sword swipes during your procession.

The Speeches: During the ceremony, the head elders will give long, drawn-out speeches full of false promises and vague suggestions about how to "make the most out of your new ninja life" and throw out a few off-topic jokes that will fall embarrassingly flat. They will, of course, ask you to find a typically ninjaesque perch for the duration of the speech segment.

The speech portion of the ceremony is also when the ninjadates first face death. During the speeches, the "assassination fellows" will attempt to kill any conspicuous ninjadates with long-range weaponry. Being well hidden and keeping up a good defense is a must. Of course, the challenge will be beating the other ninjadates to the most ideal perches.

Conferring of the Ninja Degree: Once the speech portion of the ceremony has concluded, the head elder will say something like "all ninjadates may descend from their concealed perches. We will not attempt to kill you." Don't be fooled. They will try to kill you. At this point, all dead ninjadates will simultaneously fall bloodily from their perches, while all foolish ninjas will descend noisily from theirs, only to be picked off by the assigned assassins like low-hanging mangoes. You, having read this book, will know better (if you are still alive, of course). Instead of plopping down from the tree, you must wait for the head elder to call your name, and then rappel quickly from your perch, sprint to the stage and grab the ninja degree from the head elder's clutches. Only once you are holding your degree in your hands are you truly considered part of the clan, and, therefore, safe.

✳ ✳ ✳

VALEDICTORIAN GRADUATION BATTLE

All clans conclude the ceremonies with a graduation battle, fierce competition in which they pit the class's top four ninjadates in gruesome winner-takes-all battles or long, difficult races for the distinguished mark of "top-tuna-*maki*." While each clan adopts their own variation of this sacred ninja tradition, one thing is certain: If you do not win, your parents will be less proud. The following are some examples of common valedictorian battles:

The Eat-Off: A popular variation of the Graduation Battle in America's plumper states is the old fashioned eat-off. The top ninjadates will be fed a smorgasbord of rich foods until all but one suffers a debilitating food coma and dies. The head elders will officiate, distributing the food evenly and making sure that the ninjadates continue to eat the food at an acceptable pace. **How to Win:** It's no surprise that one of the greatest hot dog eating contest competitors in the world is a ninja: An underpracticed aspect of *ninjutsu* is the Art of Accelerated Food Digestion, whereby the ninja processes the food rapidly through a series of belches, induced sweats and intense brain spasms.

The No-Eat Off: More recently, several American clans have held no eat-offs, during which the contestants stare into one another's eyes from across the room. They are forbidden from eating or drinking, and the competition is over when one of the contestants collapses (and eventually dies) from psychosis-induced kidney failure. These "battles" usually last four to five days. **How to Win:** The wise ninja always recycles. Don't sweat, spit, pee or defecate, as doing so will result in the loss of precious fluids.

The No-Limbs Battle: Often, clans will have ninjadates engage in one-on-one battles with the caveat that the competitors cannot use their limbs. After the combatants have their hands and feet tied tightly together, they are expected to fight to the death. **How to Win:** Without your arms and legs, your striking points are limited. Shoulder blades, large noses, foreheads and pointed chins can all deliver death blows, but are also extremely risky. Don't be afraid to use your mouth. A sharp bite to the ear will surprise your opponent, while a poison dart from a blowgun will kill him.

The Dizzinator: In this classic battle, ninjadates race across a deep gorge on precariously stretched tightropes *after spinning 10,000 360s.* **How to Win:** The trick here, of course, is not to fall. To do so, contestants must not get dizzy, an accomplishment that can be achieved by *spot fixation.* In spot fixation, ninjas choose one unmoving object and concentrate their gaze upon that object for the duration of their 10,000 spins.

Aquatic Races: For coastal ninja clans, the aquatic race is a very popular final battle. Ninjadates race from one destination to another (usually California or Oregon to Japan and back). Contestants may choose their form of travel, as long as it is natural. This may mean swimming, skipping or hitching a ride on migrating sea life such as dolphins, whales, great white sharks or giant jelly fish. Often, ninjadates find themselves bouncing from one migratory species to another in a technique called "baiting."

In this "battle," combat is encouraged but, considering the vastness of the ocean, rare. The most useful combat technique is to mimic the clicks of your opponent's animal's calls to convince their swimming mammals to dive to skull-crushing depths. **How to Win:** To win an aquatic race, you must balance the following three aspects of the race:

(a) *Speed.* It is a race after all. Remember, "Keep calm and swim on."

(b) *Staying fed.* Because your race will last between 20 and 400 days, you must find creative ways to stay fed. Obviously, the Art of Salt Water Digestion is a must, but so is the Art of Deep Water Fishing, Krill Katchin' and, of course, Cruise Boat Poaching.

(c) *Staying Warm.* You will begin your battle naked, and believe us, without a wet suit the waters of the Pacific are as cold as a bitchy snow leopard's icy blue stare. Early on, you will want to slay a polar bear, seal, sea lion or elephant seal and form a makeshift wet suit of its blubber for insulation.

Congratulations! If you have survived training, been accepted into a clan, survived the clan's graduation ceremony and defeated your opponent in the final battle, you are not dead! Furthermore, you are now, by recognition and mandate of the INF (International Ninja Federation), under the jurisdiction of your local ninja charter, guided by the laws, commandments and rules of propriety of the OAN (Order of American Ninjas) and within the rein of your dojo's head elders, officially a ninja! Congratulations! You did it, sir! You finished the long and painful journey to ninjahood. You have *gone ninja*.

CHAPTER 19

LIVING THE NINJA HIGH LIFE: PERKS, ACTIVITIES AND TRAVEL

NINJA PERKS

Now that you've gone ninja, you are forever part of one of the world's most celebrated societies—the ninja community. As a part of this community, you will have access to numerous private resources, both in your home town and in exotic locales abroad. This everexpanding network of deadly friends includes savvy business associates, fine restaurants and comfortable futon couches to crash on in nearly every part of the world.

ART AND CULTURE

MONA (Museum of Ninja Art): With locations in Cleveland, Ohio, College Park, Maryland, Albuquerque, New Mexico, and Kasigluk, Alaska, MONA may not be convenient for day trips, but is still a must see. In addition to permanent exhibits such as their collection of

Da Vinci's inspiration, the famous **Kunoichi of Nagano**

"Famous and Deadly Swords" sketches of "Severed Manparts," the painting *Death of a Samurai* and "Weapons: A Recollective," all four locations also offer temporary installations that have been hailed as "some of today's best stuff." The Kasigluk location has long been considered by most critics to be the crème de la crème, with a host of groundbreaking temporary installments such as "Anatomy: Severed Limbs and Disemboweled Organs" and their recent modern art installment entitled "Post-Beheading Spray, 1990–2000."

Ninja! The Musical: Step aside, *Cats* and *Wicked*, the ninjas have taken the stage. Entering its seventh consecutive year on Broadway and winner of 12 Tony Awards including Best Swordfight Choreography and Most Dangerous Musical to Watch. *Ninja! The Musical* is "a real hoot for the whole ninja family." Directed by Ms. Glen Beck (*The American Samurai in Tokyo*) and with set and costume design by famed designer Lauren Smack (*Tempura My Heart*), the musical has been hailed as "the ultimate representation of ninja drama, comedy, fight choreography and ninja-on-ninja sex."

THE NINJA LINE (212) 456-1414

With 24-hour service, an easy-to-find number, and friendly offshore specialists waiting to assist you in any way they can, The Ninja Line is a vital resource for every beginning ninja. The Ninja Line's capable specialists will assist you with any ninja-related inquiry or problem, from "how to properly assist a dying pet with *seppuku*," to "correctly rolling a poisoned Philly roll." The Ninja Line should be number 1 on every ninja's speed dial. When you call the number, the operator will inform you that you've reached the switchboard for the White House in Washington D.C. Simply say, "*Arigato,*" and ask to speak with your local ninja representative, ending with, "And please give my regards to *Sama* (Mr.) President."

ONLINE RESOURCES

Ninjanewswire.com: "All the news that's fit to punch." Ninjanewswire.com is the highest-ranked source for ninja-related headlines in the world.

ninjamatchmaker.com: At the forefront of Internet dating is the wildly popular ninjamatchmaker.com. The "innovative" and "user-friendly" ninja social networking site plays host to about 80 percent of today's young, single ninja population, as well as an estimated three million ninja wannabes and ninja groupies. Not just for the single ninja on the prowl, ninjamatchmaker.com is also a great way to stay connected with cohorts, friends and relatives without divulging the personal information that would get you killed.

Ninjas-n-couches.com: Equally perfect for the backpacking ninja or the business on assignment ninja abroad, ninjas-n-couches.com is a vital traveling resource that specializes in connecting eager ninja interns, couch-surfing crash pads and post-assassination getaway carpools. After generations of ninja secrecy, this site is seen as an example of the ninja community's budding altruistic tendencies.

Kamikaze.net: By far the planet's most reliable weather forecast site, this is the go-to spot to find out what the weather will be like in your assigned city today, tomorrow and this date in the year 2020. Every good ninja knows that unexpected weather can ruin the best laid assassination plans, so check your cold fronts today.

RETAIL AND SHOPPING

Sexy Dark: This beauty parlor chain, with locations in over 50 American cities, has been whipping up ninja facials and mani-pedies since 1981. Ideal for ninja clans not practiced in the arts of disguise and impersonation, Sexy Dark specializes in top-to-bottom disguise transformations that are guaranteed to fool the enemy. Choose from a classic disguise (bum, traveling monk, whore) or modern one (hipster, hippy, yuppie), or for a more personalized transformation, purchase the "design your own" makeover option. Known more for its excellent disguise makeovers rather than sparkling customer service, don't expect the Vietnamese *kunoichi* that run the parlor to flatter you by speaking English, and when they laugh, rest assured that yes, they *are* laughing at you.

Trader Joji's: Specializing in everything from 36-hour energy drinks and high-protein bull testicles to organic vegetables and fine sake,

Trader Joji's is the one-stop shop for all your dojo and battlefield dietary needs.

Whole Foods & Swords: While Whole Foods & Swords is significantly more expensive than stores like Trader Joji's and Stab and Save, it offers an unparalleled assortment of fair-trade battle items, including weaponry, armor, rope ladders and camouflage makeup. Furthermore, all the food and products are made from organically grown plants and animals, which means that their chickens, pigs, cows, polar bears and dolphins had a fantastic life before being beheaded by a ninja sword and sliced into delicious bite-size pieces that are then shrinkwrapped in biodegradable plastic. So you don't have to feel guilty when you spend half your paycheck on one week's supply of food.

The Inkjet Vagabonds: A temp agency for *ninjutsu* related services, the Inkjet Vagabonds are a collection of "unbound ninjas" (ninjas who don't belong to any clan or dojo) who will work "any assignment for any clan, if the pay is right." Vagabonds may be expensive, but they are good at what they do. Of course, you will not need to contact the Inkjet Vagabonds until you reach the managerial levels of your clan, which usually takes between three months and 70 years.

IKEA: A great resource for any first-time ninja homeowner, IKEA offers sleek, simple furniture and home furnishings that are easy to assemble and very affordable!

LEGAL DEFENSE

Marty Leibowitz-Hashuya, Esq.: Ninjas, whether they want to believe it or not, are bound by the laws of the country in which they operate. Assassinations and breaking and entering, both integral parts of the ninja's day-to-day life, are extremely illegal in the United States, and having access to a good lawyer is essential for any ninja operating within the continental U.S. Considered the best ninja lawyer in America, Leibowitz-Hashuya has been helping ninjas get out of legal jams since 1971, when he graduated from Harvard Law School with a focus on Constitutional and Ninja Law. While his prices are certainly exorbitant ($500 per hour, per member of his research team), his services are matchless. According to one resource, no judge has ever convicted a ninja represented by Leibowitz-Hashuya. *Important Tip:* Don't try to stiff Marty on the fee; he keeps a clan of superadvanced ninjas on his payroll.

The NCLU (Ninja Civil Liberties Union): Set up to defend the individual battle rights afforded to any ninja under the constitution and laws of the United States, the NCLU, a spinoff of the ACLU, has been helping disenfranchised minority ninja groups since 1950.

HIDDEN NINJA TRAVEL

Kenji's Seaside Bungalows, Vancouver Island, Canada: The "Great Ninja Migration" of the late 1970s saw tens of thousands of ninja masters emigrate from the U.S. to Canada. Today, bustling ninja communities on the Ucluelet Peninsula, just outside Vancouver, have become tourist magnets for urban ninjas looking for a peaceful immersion into the traditional ninja life. Perched on beautifully rugged Vancouver Island, this string of quaint ninja towns offers a breathtaking mix of old Japan and grand Victorian elegance. The highlight of a trip to the area is a lengthy stay at Kenji's Seaside Bungalows, which offers a host of ninja- and family-friendly amenities like in-room rice cookers and seaweed drying racks, as well as a bevy of exciting activities from fishing and archery to exhilarating killer whale rides.

❉ ❉ ❉

NINJA ACTIVITIES

Like all Americans, American Ninja Converts have short attention spans and a constant desire for diversions. But ninjas are too athletic for slow-pitch softball, too smart for YouTube videos and too musically inept for concerts. The following activities are particularly popular among American ninjas.

FUN WITH GREAT WHITE SHARKS

Born in the Pacific-locked islands of Japan, *ninjutsu* shares a deep and unbreakable bond with the creatures of the deep. One fish held in particular esteem is the playful, toothy great white shark! For centuries, coastal ninja clans carefully bred these killing machines by mating small, docile reef sharks with vicious megaladon giants.

Due to their keen sense of smell and electromagnetic perception, early sharks were raised as helpful hunting pets to aid the ninja's fishing adventures and earned the catchy nickname "ninja sailor's best white friend." Finally, during the Great Fishing Recession of the 17th century, the expansive great white farms were sunk and the once-domesticated sharks left to roam the vast oceans alone.

Freediving with Great Whites: Today, the sport of free diving with great whites continues to be a favorite ninja pastime and an excellent training method for beginning ninjas. By slicing a fledgling ninja's wrist and tossing him into infested waters, the clans induce widespread bloodlust as the sharks go into "feeding frenzy" mode. Most ninjas can expect to lose a limb or at least a finger or two during each of their first several free dives, but by the time you learn to evade a school of bloodthirsty great whites, you'll be quick and clever enough to evade the wiliest of human foes.

Great White Bareback Riding: A more humane way of interacting with these natural ninja comrades is the emerging sport of Great White Bareback Riding. Capable of reaching speeds in excess of 25 miles per hour, the sharks make a great mode of transportation either for weekend fun or covert business travel.

NINJA SPORTS AND GAMES

For generations, ninjas have found ways of making their endless training regiments more enjoyable. Today, many American clans have ninjafied several classic American recreational games and sports.

Croquet: Oft considered the "warrior's sport," croquet encompasses a wide range of ninja training tactics, including hand-eye coordination, concentration, cruelty and backstabbing. Of course the ninja variation is much more violent and faster-paced than the classic version. Ninjas are allowed to use their mallets as bludgeons and the pegs as projectiles to disorient or disable their opponents, and wrestling matches often ensue during more epic croquet battles.

Twister: The annual Ninja Twister Tournament, held in Boise, Idaho, is one of the most benign and respected ninjas competitions that take place in the States. The tournament includes both "traditional Twister" and "ninja Twister," both with weapons and non-weapons versions. Ninja Twister, of course, is played with more, smaller dots, upward-facing rusted nails and more body parts, so that "right nostril fuchsia" or "inner abdomen mauve" are just as common commands as "right foot red" or "left hand yellow."

Hide and Go Seek (for Ninjas): For the youthful or nostalgic ninja, hide and go seek (for ninjas) is an excellent way to train concealment techniques while having a real blast! Hide and go seek (for ninjas) can be played in the woods or in a house, in a kelp forest or on small archipelago. Of course, hide and go seek (for ninjas) differs slightly from conventional hide and go seek (for laymen) in that the ninja version includes "ninja tagging," a slightly more violent version of tagging in which the ninja who is "it" must not just find the hiders but also lightly stab them in the abdomen with a small pin. Expert hide and go seekers implement diversion techniques such as smoke bombs, holograms or voice throwing.

Paintball (with *Yumi*): Many ninja clans bond by hosting the occasional paintball match. Of course, ninjas don't use anything quite so painless as balls of paint; instead, they use *yumi* (ninja bows and arrows), using arrows that have slightly duller-than-usual tips, ensuring that the puncture wound will not be too deep. There are paintball courses in nearly every American region; unfortunately, most paintball courses don't allow players to use *yumi*. Instead, go after dark, when the courses are unattended. You may have to deal with a security guard or two, but the fun you and your friends will have will be well worth the hassle!

CHAPTER 20

NINJA DATING

In an age of technologically induced isolation, long work weeks and disconnected societies, finding a date can be a challenge. For the ninja, it can feel nearly impossible. Whether you're trying to fit in a quick dinner date between missions or attempting to explain your detailed profession to a jaded Brooklyn hipster, finding love in this steel-sharpened world may make you want to commit *seppuku*.

So where did all the ninja's sexual allure go? Weren't you sold on a bill of money, intrigue and multiple sexual partners? Do not fret, young ninja, a wide world of ninja love exists just below the surface.

✾ ✾ ✾

WHERE TO MEET NINJOPHILE MATES

After extensive research, the authors have found that the following several places/activities are among the most fertile hunting grounds for potential mates:

Yogalates: If you're a male ninja on the prowl for a date, your local yoga/Pilates combination class offers a great way to slaughter two birds with one well-flung *shuriken*. With an average girl-to-guy ratio of four-to-one, yogalates classes are excellent places for male ninjas to go girl-hunting while working on dexterity and strengthening the core. Be wary, of course, of weird hippies who believe in astrology and think that inanimate objects can "be blessed" and therefore "hold positive energy," as they tend to both frequent yogalates classes and have a corrupting peaceful influence on ninjas.

Dog and Tiger Parks: It's a fact—everyone loves cute and cuddly things. If you consider that people with pets are pretty much always single, than you'll realize why your local animal run is a goldmine for potential dates. Of course, you will look like a creep if you go to a "dog" park unadorned: Bring your pet tiger! Cute, fuzzy, cuddly, and sporting an eye-catching coat, your tiger will let available hotties know that you're sweet but also mean business. Keep your tiger leashed, even in a large dog run, as grown tigers and dogs tend to play a bit too rough.

Take your cuddly tiger to your local dog and tiger park to meet other animal lovers.

Fro-Mo Shops (Frozen Mochi Shops): Perhaps nothing assuages loneliness more than a dollop or two of doughy ice cream mochi. And these supertrendy fro-mo shops are popping up everywhere, attracting ninjas, ninjophiles and foodies alike. So head down to your local fro-mo shop for delicious treats and charming banter with local patrons.

A BRIEF NOTE ON INTERCOURSE

Ninjas have been enjoying this classic activity since early in their inception. To engage in intercourse, simply find a willing partner and go at it. Remember, though, not all non-ninjas enjoy advanced positions and moves such as the "wild mushroom," "the rusted tornado" or "the meditative sloth." When intercoursing for the first time with a new non-ninja partner, remember, "*communication* is the key to *stimulation*."

❀ ❀ ❀

NINJA PICK-UPS FROM THE NINJA DATING EXPERTS

Your new status as a ninja does afford you some serious advantages when making your way through the singles' scene. Your all-black attire and chic headwear makes the self-assured claim that "ninja is the new black." The key to your social success is playing up the ninja through a direct, confident approach. Try the following lines (in English or Japanese) the next time you're out:

THE NO NONSENSE NINJA APPROACH

Hey, you're cute.

Nē, kawaiidesu.

This standard, straightforward line indicates that you have used your keen ninja senses to notice your future conquest. The matter-of-fact aggressiveness of the statement lets that "cute" individual know that you're in charge and you know what's going on in the world. The fact that you're pointing your drawn blade at them is also a bold indication of just how much business you really mean.

COMPLEX STATEMENT
WITH SUBTLE DOUBLE MEANING

I'd like a stab at you! Metaphorically, I mean. Sorry, it's a ninja thing.

Watashi wa anata ni sasu yō ni onegai shimasu. Hiyu-teki ni, watashi wa imi shimasu. Watashi wa ninja o shite imasu.

Humor! Not only have you made a joke out of double meaning, but you've slyly managed to sneak in the fact that you're a ninja in a bumbling, Hugh Grant sort of way. It's the perfect ploy and probably has your target mate drooling right about now.

A STANDARD OFFER PAIRED
WITH A DARK NINJA PROPOSAL

Could I buy you a drink or let you touch my sword?

Watashi wa o sake o kōnyu shi tari, anata ga watashi no ken o sawara sete moraemasu ka?

You show your sweet side with the drink offer. Then *BAM*, this innocent offer has become a delicate hint that next to your stacked wallet is a dark, sharp and dangerous side. What did you mean by "sword" anyway? You've just blown open the door of mystery into which that curious someone can't help but wander.

CHAPTER 21

GETTING NINJA WORK

GOING NINJA FREELANCER

"Everybody's killing for the weekend."

—Talloned Loverboy Ryu, c. 15th century

Your adventure toward complete ninjahood has been memorable. In fact, it's probably been the best time in your life. Training day and night over the last couple of months, you've managed to chisel that once pear-shaped body into a smooth Doric column. You've transformed your soft, vulnerable hands into tools of lethal destruction. And you've honed your mind, rearranging the clunky neural pathways into streamlined broadband synapses. You've battled thugs, vagabonds and other ninjas and discovered the many joys of white rice. You've made the transition. Now it's time to put your new status to work.

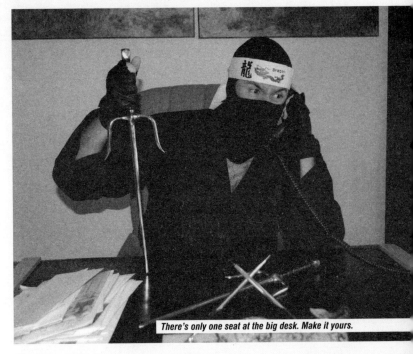

There's only one seat at the big desk. Make it yours.

If you've chosen to join up with a unionized ninja clan, you're probably set for life when it comes to catching missions and getting bankrolled. Sure, you're looking at years of hazing and grunt work, but in the end the ninja clan is a solid way to earn a living.

For those of you who have chosen to forgo the clan lifestyle and strike out as an independent contractor, you've got a bit of work ahead of you. The payoff, however is just as appealing. Being your own ninja boss is an amazing way to earn a living.

Your first task is figuring out what type of ninja you plan on being. Get started by filling in the following simple career quiz.

TEN SIMPLE QUESTIONS TO A NINJA CAREER

1. When breaking boards with my head ____________________
   (a) I often get a headache.
   (b) I like to save the pieces.
   (c) I typically forget to remove the sleeping kitten.

2. When I spill a glass of milk ____________________
   (a) I weep uncontrollably.
   (b) I clean it up and move on.
   (c) I kill the cow that made it.

3. I imagine the loss of this organ to be most upsetting:
   (a) Heart
   (b) Skin
   (c) Brain

4. Around teardrops I feel ____________________
   (a) empathy.
   (b) queasy.
   (c) enraged.

5. The pen is ____________________ than the sword.
   (a) mightier
   (b) duller
   (c) stealthier

6. In a romantic relationship, I am typically looking for _____
    (a) deep connection.
    (b) hot sex.
    (c) cold revenge.

7. Newborn babies are _____
    (a) adorable.
    (b) laughable.
    (c) throwable.

8. I use my _____ to shave in the morning.
    (a) razor
    (b) *ninja-to*
    (c) serrated fingernails

9. Blood is _____ than water.
    (a) yuckier
    (b) thicker
    (c) tastier

10. I will sleep when _____
    (a) I'm tired.
    (b) I'm dead.
    (c) you're dead.

THE ANSWER YOU'VE BEEN WAITING FOR

To find your future career, add up your cumulative score. For every question you answered A, add 1 point; for every B, add 2 points; for every C, add 3 points. Your future is one of the following 8 professions.

8–10 *Ninja Nanny:* Congratulations! Your answers have shown that you have a breathtakingly sensitive personality and a magical heart. However, this means that true ninja work will not suit you. Instead, you may want to advertise your services as a ninja nanny. Ninjas are often away on missions and are always looking for a trustworthy babysitter!

11–13 *Assistant Ninja Costume Designer:* Congratulations! Your answers reveal that you have a deep understanding of the human condition, a creative outlook and admirable dexterity. As such, you should avoid any violent ninja work, seeking instead to work for a clan as its assistant costume designer.

14–16 *Ninja Book Editor:* Congratulations! Your answers indicate a moderate capacity for theoretical violence, but a deep intolerance for any actual gore. Your intellectual outlook and conceptual understanding of violence will help you succeed as an editor for ninja instruction manuals, guidebooks and blogs.

17–19 *Sushi Chef:* Congratulations! According to your answer choices, you have an icy temperament, decent sword skills, and a slight capacity for murder. Unfortunately, you value human life, meaning that you're better suited for slaughtering lower-strata beings such as *ika* (squid) or *maguro* (tuna). Take your sword to your local sushi restaurant and start chopping!

20–22 *Karate Teacher:* Congratulations! Your answer choices reveal that while you have a capacity for violence, you still become queasy at the thought of getting real blood on your hands. Take your talents to your local karate dojo and recruit impressionable 12 year olds to learn the skills you'll never quite master.

23–25 *Ninja Clan Occupational Therapist:* Congratulations! Topics like dismemberment, enucleation, beheading and murder excite you. However, while you do possess the requisite enthusiasm to be a ninja assassin, you also have the tiniest seed of doubt that will tug at your heartstrings every time you try to commit a murder. Instead of seeking work as an assassin, seek employment as an occupational therapist for your local clan.

26–29 *Mid-Level Ninja Clansman:* Congratulations! You have a very rare mental capacity for *being* involved in assassination, which will secure you a position as a mid-level ninja clansman. Unfortunately, you do not possess the utter heartlessness required to lead a clan or subclan of your own. Middle management should be your top rung!

30 *Cold-Blooded Ninja Assassin:* Congratulations! Your answers indicate that you fall in the most badass sociopathic category of ninja warrior. The cold-blooded ninja assassin. Your new nine-to-five will leave many a soul six feet under.

QUITTING YOUR CURRENT JOB

Accountant by day, ninja by night? Not going to happen. Ninja work takes time, and being a fully employed ninja means devoting your entire life to your work. Some assignments—like dispatching a pesky squirrel your mom has been complaining about—take mere minutes. But others can last for weeks, months, or even years. Prolonged espionage missions, for example, often require around-the-clock observation of a target, and catalyzing a government upheaval often results in full-scale war, which can last as long as two or three months, sometimes even four. With the average ninja assignment lasting a little over three weeks, you simply cannot afford to have another job.

Quitting a job is a scary proposition, especially in today's economy. What if I don't find ninja work? you may ask yourself. What if the ninja work I do receive is not as lucrative as my current job? Hush, *panku*. Ninjas don't ask questions, they answer them.

Make sure you go out with a maximum of flamboyancy but a minimum of bloodshed, for legal reasons.

ADVERTISING YOUR NEW POSITION

Being a self-employed ninja means drumming up your own clients. Without a savvy marketing strategy, your client list will remain about as short as the bloody tip of a spent ninja star. But if you brand yourself correctly, come up with a viable, cost-effective and original marketing strategy, and focus your efforts on target areas and niche demographics, you will see your client list quickly become as long as your unsheathed sword.

Missed Connections: While you may not think it, the occasional Missed Connection posted online can land you a solid job.

Saw You on the L Train—m4w (Brooklyn)

Hey, this is to the beautiful 20-something brunette on the L last Friday night around midnight.

Billboards are an excellent way to reach several commuters every day. To catch a driver's eye, you should probably have several half-naked women on your billboard. Sure, it has nothing to do with your ninja services, but so what?

We made eye-contact (a few times!). You were wearing a flowy lavender summer dress; I was wearing all black and carrying swords/groceries.

I don't know if this is too forward, but you seemed pissed at your bf (probably cheating or not appreciating you). Anyway, let me know if you're looking for some ninja advice—I'm really good at assassination! Or maybe we could just get a coffee.

I'd love to help.

Urinal Cakes: Urinal cakes are an effective and cost-efficient way of targeting male clients. Furthermore, most men are feeling very insecure and vulnerable while peeing in urinals because they are staring at their penises, and only 2 percent of men are confident with their flaccid penises hanging out. As you know, insecure and vulnerable people are more likely to hire ninjas.

Viral Videos: With your brand-spanking-new, incredibly amazing ninja skills, you should have no problem creating a viral video sensation. Past ninjas sensations include: "Ghost Ride the Dolphin," "Ninja Climbs a Ladder Using His Penis," "Giggling Baby Dodges *Shuriken*," "Sneezing *Tanuki* Drums His Testicles [sick beat]" and "It Is My Genitalia inside of a Sword Sheath (Happy Fourth of July, Baby)."

NETWORKING

One of the quickest ways to obtain clients is by tapping into your existing social networks. A mass social-networking message is a good start, but do you really think your online friends have the budget to hire you for ninja services? Instead, hack into your mother's e-mail account and send a message to all of her contacts. Middle-aged and elderly people are more likely to help for three reasons. First, they have more money. Second, they've lived longer and therefore have accrued more significant grudges. And third, they find it pleasurable to help out their friends' children. When constructing your e-mail, feel free to use the following rubric:

Dear friends, family and coworkers of my mom,

I hope this e-mail finds you well.

As many of you know, I've been training to become a professional ninja for several weeks now. It's been an exciting journey, and I've learned many new and useful skills. Unfortunately, the fun and games are officially over, as it's time for me to start looking for gainful ninja employment.

Like any profession, becoming a ninja is accompanied by a long, arduous career path. And unfortunately, today, most ninjas wallow in filth and poverty for months before building a high-quality curriculum vitae to establish a reputation. As I am new to the job, I need all the help I can get from friends and family.

What can you do?

Hire me for any short-term ninja-related jobs you might have. Perhaps you have someone you would like to set up surveillance on? Maybe you have an imminent sushi-themed cocktail party and can't find a chef on such short notice? Maybe you have shrubbery that could use a clean whack with a sharp sword? Or perhaps, and this will be between us, you have someone you might like to have disappear for a bit.

I don't have any references as of yet, but I would be happy to personally demonstrate some of my more impressive ninja skills.

Anyway, feel free to e-mail or call me. My rates are reasonable and negotiable, and I promise my services will delight.

Thank you for your consideration, and I hope to see all of you soon.

Sincerely,

[Insert ninja name here]

[Insert given name here]

NINJA PRODUCTS

With a growing young ninja demographic, coming up with a ninja-friendly product can be a great way to earn a living. Creating a marketable product takes ingenuity, but American ninjas are always looking for the next hot ninja trend. One of the most popular ninja products to date, of course, is the ShuriPod, a metallic MP3 player replete with sharpened blades. Another top product is the Ninja Snuggles, the comfortable fleece onesie that keeps you warm, comfortable and fully armed on the battlefield as well as in the bedroom.

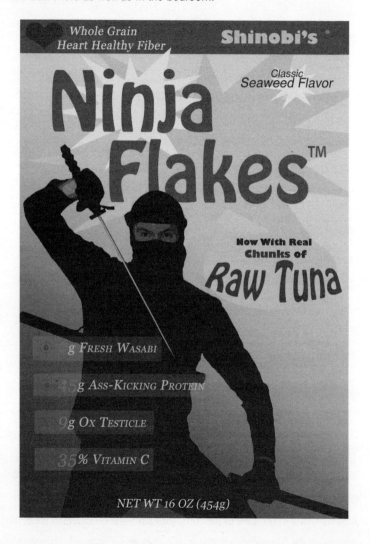

✳ ✳ ✳

TRADITIONAL NINJA WORK

BEGGING

In the midst of a crippling recession, "luxury services" like espionage and assassination are not as popular as they once were. If you find yourself unable to get work, you may want to resort to begging on the street. With a simple yet informative sign, a calculated look of puppy-dog despair and a coffee cup large enough to fit silver dollars, you will either get hired for ninja services, or make about $2.13 per hour.

INTIMIDATING SERVICES

While you're waiting for higher-paying, more exciting ninja-related work, why not make a couple extra quarters by taking simpler jobs? Intimidation services account for a high percentage of most ninjas' bankrolls during their first year of work, as they are among the safest ninja jobs and require the least amount of experience.

Relatively low on the danger scale and chock-full of potential clients, an easy place to perform your first intimidation mission is at your neighborhood elementary school, where you can earn a small fortune in milk money by counter-bullying class bullies.

Once you get comfortable intimidating children, you will be ready to move on to adults. Fortunately for the ninja, statistics show that every adult has at least one formidable enemy. While most Americans are not willing to have their enemies assassinated, a little bloodless revenge is always welcome. For you, this means that *everybody* is a potential client. Keep your ears and eyes open at all times, watching every interaction for signs of hatred or disharmony.

ESPIONAGE

Espionage is the most adventurous ninja related service you can hope to get into. With relatively few moral dilemmas, a minimum of bloodshed and little physical confrontation, the spy game is also easier than your assassination or intimidation gigs. Furthermore, it comes with a much better ruse—private investigator—than disguises used in more violent professions, such as cleaner, sanitation worker or banana hammock salesman.

❊ ❊ ❊

WORKING YOUR WAY
UP THE KILLING LADDER

Before you ever consider what it would be like to take another life, you should work your way up the killing ladder. The following five steps will put you on the assassin's path in no time flat.

Step 1—Killing the Last of the Milk: Killing a carton of milk may seem innocuous, but what if that carton were your best friend's? Or better yet, what if it were not only your best friend's milk but also the only thing preventing him from developing a debilitating case of osteoporosis just 40 years from now? That's some seriously cold-blooded, dairy-style murder.

Step 2—Killing the Lights: Killing the lights, of course, takes only a minimum of icy heartlessness. To make this rung more challenging, try killing the lights at inconvenient times, such as the middle of a wedding speech or at a high-traffic intersection.

Step 3—Killing the Mood: Killing the mood is a bit colder-blooded than killing the lights, but not by much. There are several surefire ways of killing the mood, which range from the more general "being a downer" to the more specific "announcing you have contagious airborne syphilis at an orgy." Remember, the more elevated the mood, the harder it is to kill it. The true ninja practices killing the mood by doing it in really happy environments, such as at baby showers, romantic comedies or birthday parties.

Step 4—Killing Two Birds with One Stone: This fourth rung elevates your cold-blooded killing quotient to a new level, as it is the first at which you will be asked to kill an organic being. Killing two birds with one stone tests a wide range of ethical frigidity; taking out two red-breasted robins is one thing, but killing two eagles? Not only does that symbolically suggest that you hate America, but you are also killing two highly evolved creatures with a capacity for love and monogamy.

Step 5—Killing Time: This final rung is perhaps more morally insipid than killing human beings, as it requires destroying the laws of physics, which are major tenants of science, which is akin to religion for hundreds of millions of people. Killing time will put the world into a tailspin, both figuratively and literally.

CONCLUSION

YOUR PLACE IN THE FUTURE NINJA GLOBAL DOMINATION

Look at you, ninja! I mean, seriously, look at you. Put down the book, right now, walk straight into the bathroom and stare in the mirror. Are you looking? Steal a glance at your mysterious new face and rippling ninja body. Pretty sexy stuff, huh? Your formerly ruddy chipmunk-cheeked face has been replaced with a strong, square jaw, pronounced cheekbones and icy eyes. Notice how your forehead muscles have nearly doubled in size? You are a veritable don of badassery.

Now find a full-body mirror. Strip off your clothes. (No, not all of them, for ninja's sake. Leave your ninja tighty-whities *on*. You never know when an attack might come, and having to kill someone naked would be embarrassing, to say the least.) Quite a change, wouldn't you say? Where there once were small muscles and large fat deposits, perhaps a few varicose veins and stretch marks, now sit sinewy muscles and calcium-hardened bones that protrude like the rigid roots of a gnarled oak. It's true; you are, for the first time in your life, sexy. Go ahead and say it to yourself. Look in the mirror and utter the following mantra: *"I am a ninja, and I am damn sexy."*

But not only that: You finished an *entire* book. Granted, there were a number of photos and pictures throughout this fine piece of instructional literature, but still, all that paper is nothing to sneeze at. If you need to sneeze right now, that's fine, just don't sneeze at your accomplishments. Remember, "The ninja who holds in his sneezes will die in battle because he will sneeze during an inopportune moment." It's better to let out your sneeze right now, when you're reading a book, rather than later, when you are engaged in a ninja death battle.

And the awesomeness doesn't stop there! Not only are you sexier and better read than before you picked up this book, but you are also a full-fledged ninja! You know the secrets of the greatest tradition in the history of the world. A cold-blooded killing machine, that's what you've become. Do a cartwheel. Awesome! Make a fist. Holy *shuriken*! Draw your *ninja-to* and slash something up with vigor. Disgusting!

✸ ✸ ✸

A WORD TO THE NINJA TOURISTS

Prior to publication, a "friend" offered to *read* the book. When he finished, he said that he thought it "was a comprehensive, solid addition to the ninja canon." We asked how he found the training regimen outlined in the book's pages. The "friend" replied that he had simply *read* the book; he had not followed our foolproof four-week training plan. He had not gone on the Ninja Battle Diet, done any of the exercises, completed a single cartwheel, or killed *anything*. We had given him the keys to ninjahood and he had thrown them in the ocean, choosing instead to merely *imagine* what it *might be like* to be a ninja.

We are aware that several readers currently perusing this page have taken a similar approach to this book. To you, ninja tourists, we have one message: You are a terrible human being.

Because you're American, and Americans always get a second chance in life, we're willing to give you one. Relax your shoulders; take a deep breath. Now flip the book back to the first page and start over.

For those who have completed this program and gone ninja, congratulations, we are proud of you. You have taken the first step in what will be a lifetime of exhausting walking. Today, more than ever before, it is vital that every ninja dedicate himself to the ninja cause. In America, we ninjas are at a pivotal crossroads. On one fork lies a path paved in the golden freedom of the American ninja community. In the other direction, however, lies the bleak, pothole-laden road of oppression and darkness not unlike what followed the Great Ninja Backlash we experienced in this country 200 years ago.

You see, the American government is perpetrating an evil so vile that we were afraid to mention it earlier. You had not yet completed the ninja training program, so yours was a feeble brain of glasslike fragility. If we had told you truth too early along the path, who knows what would have happened to you. You may have cried. Certainly you would have fainted. And there's a good chance you would have quit your training. So we sugarcoated the reality, offering you a partial truth.

We told you that, with the exception of Maine, no state recognizes *ninjutsu* as a legitimate way of life, and that as a consequence, ninjas throughout the nation have almost no rights.

Our rights are being trampled upon. Not only are ninjas denied the right to assassinate, we are not allowed to participate in normal ninja lifestyles—walking our tigers, throwing *shurikens* in our local playgrounds or sharpening our swords on commercial plane flights. This oppression is, in a word, oppressive. All this you probably know. Chances are you are already outraged. But our situation is even grimmer. Throughout America, anti-ninja sentiments are reaching a boiling point, which are threatening the continued existence of the ninja.

To understand our current plight, imagine the American Ninja Community as the *Titanic*, and then imagine the American government as an iceberg replete with 100 starving polar bears, directly in the path of the mighty ship that is the American Ninja Community.

You see, the hatred for the ninja is so thorough that, over the past decade, the government has poured money into the anti-ninja lobby and numerous secret anti-ninja operations. It is our job to counteract these shady dealings. It is our duty as ninjas to overcome them.

✳ ✳ ✳

A BRIGHTER FUTURE FOR AMERICAN NINJAS

Imagine a future where every ninja is allowed the Right to Assassination, the Right to Own Tigers and the Right to Break into People's Houses for the Purposes of Espionage (cumulatively known as the holy trinity of American ninja amendments). Unless you live in Maine, such a profound paradigm shift probably seems impossible. But it is not.

In fact, most American ninjas don't simply want a few amendments; they want an entire country filled with ninjas. The American Ninja

Federation has proposed the following timetable for achieving crucial ninja landmarks:

LEGALIZED NINJAS: THE 100-YEAR PLAN

2015—Legalization of Pygmy Ninja Pets: As proposed, American ninjas will be permitted to own and house up to 10 tigers, lions, kangaroos, elephants and any other domestic animal.

2020—Legalization of Non-Infiltration Espionage: As proposed, American ninjas would be permitted to spy on any target, at any time, so long as they do not physically enter said target's property.

2025—Ninja in the House: A ninja will be elected to the United States House of Representatives.

2026—Legalization of Infiltration: Ninjas will be able to break into any house, apartment, condo, gazebo or any other property, at any time, by any means, for any reason whatsoever.

2030—Legalization of Full-Sized Ninja Pets: As proposed, American ninjas would be permitted to own and house up to 100 full-sized pets, including snow leopards, giraffes, dolphins, sharks, colossal squid and giant barking spiders.

2035—Ninjas will take the House of Representatives.

2040—One-quarter of all Americans will be ninjas.

2045—Ninjas Will Take the Congress.

2050—Legalization of Assassination: Ninjas will be allowed to assassinate whomsoever they choose for any reason whatsoever.

2075—A Ninja President: Americans will elect the country's first official ninja president.

2090—American ninjas will declare war on all nations but Japan.

2110—Every American will be a ninja.

Shifting the sands of American sentiment will not occur overnight. It will take the coordinated, sustained efforts of every last American ninja. It will take *your* help.

✳ ✳ ✳

WHAT YOU CAN DO: FOUR SIMPLE STEPS TO HELP ACHIEVE GLOBAL NINJA DOMINATION

Do your part to convince the average Americans around you that not only is America better off with ninjas, but ninjas are the key to this country's continued prosperity and power.

1. Convert Friends and Family: The more ninjas the merrier! The first step toward erasing America's anti-ninja sentiments is to convince as many people as possible to become American Ninja Converts. Tell your friends and family members how amazing your ninja life is; show them kick-ass cartwheels and reveal your washboard abdomen muscles. They will convert.

2. Write to Your Local Representative: Write a letter to your local representative telling him that you are a ninja and you will not vote for him if he doesn't support ninja rights.

3. Make Awesome Videos for YouTube / Make Awesome Facebook Groups: Telling your friends and family members is a start, what about communities in which no ninjas are operating? The best way to reach these "dead zones" is to create an awesome viral video or create an awesome Facebook groups.

4. Volunteer: Grassroots efforts are the final step to erasing America's anti-ninja sentiments. Volunteer to canvas for the Ninja Civil Liberties Union (NCLU) or any local ninja organization that fundraises on behalf of the NCLU. Hit the streets, knock on doors, do whatever it takes to raise awareness and money in support of the ninja cause.

✱ ✱ ✱

CONCLUSION OF THE CONCLUSION

That's about it, ninja. You've done it all! You've transformed yourself from a chubby white-collar idiot into a sharp-brained, sharper-bodied ninja, and you've joined the national ninja movement. The authors would like to thank you in advance for your participation in the upcoming ninja revolution.

We'll see you on the battlefield.

—Sam the Sinewy and Glorious Manparts Keith

PHOTO CREDITS

OTHER ULYSSES PRESS BOOKS

When Ninjas Attack: A Survival Guide for Defending Yourself Against the Silent Assassins

Sam Kaplan, Phoebe Bronstein & Keith Riegert, $12.95

Death waits around every corner for the unprepared American. Luckily, this book reveals the vital information one needs to identify, outwit and counter-strike against these black-masked killers.

Dirty Japanese: Everyday Slang from "What's Up?" to "F*%# Off!"

Matt Fargo, $10.00

Even in traditionally minded Japan, slang from its edgy pop culture constantly enters into common usage. *Dirty Japanese* fills in the gap between how people really talk in Japan and what Japanese-language students are taught.

Zombiewood Weekly: The Celebrity Dead Exposed

Rob Sacchetto, $14.95

In this paparazzi-inspired collection of images, America's bad and beautiful are revealed as never before—in their undisguised, flesh-rotting, zombified, day-to-day existence.

To order these books call 800-377-2542 or 510-601-8301, fax 510-601-8307, e-mail ulysses@ulyssespress.com, or write to Ulysses Press, P.O. Box 3440, Berkeley, CA 94703. All retail orders are shipped free of charge. California residents must include sales tax. Allow two to three weeks for delivery.

ACKNOWLEDGMENTS

FROM SAM KAPLAN
(SAM THE SINEWY)

First and foremost I would like to thank my mother and my father; without you, I would never have learned how to fabricate a believable lie. Second, I would like to thank my younger brother, Jesse, for being a wonderful training partner throughout my life; you may be able to beat me in a game of basketball or croquet, but that's only because you insist that I put away my ninja weapons for the entire duration of the game.

There are several ninjas without whose guidance I wouldn't be the successful ninja I am today: Barbeque Bill, without your innovative use of using kitchen utensils I would still be a slave to traditional weaponry; Suzanne the Ram, thanks for the swimming and dolphin-riding lessons; Snow Leopard Man, thank you for exposing me to the wonderful world of cooking rice. And a big thank you to the entire Dirty Pants Ninja clan, especially Phil the Filthy; I couldn't imagine being a member of any other ninja union. I love each and every one of you.

Finally, I would like to thank my sparring and writing partner, Keith, for his subtle blend of encouragement and criticism. Keith, you have helped me mature as both a ninja and a writer.

FROM GLORIOUS MANPARTS KEITH

I would like to thank my personal trainer/sensei, Panda Paws Paul, for all of his guidance and brutal training. My eternal gratitude to my parents for their unwavering support over the last couple of years of ninja development, flesh wounds and a host of complicated assault charges. To my pet tiger, Toast, for his love, devotion and excessive aggression toward strangers.

A special thanks to my sister, Alice, and brother-in-law, Jadson, for their help starting the new Cuddly Bear Hug jiu-jitsu, *ninjutsu* and capoeira training facility. To Sam, for being a stellar writing partner and for never surpassing me in ninja skill. And to Lauren, for being the most dazzling creator of ninja couture on the planet.

ABOUT THE AUTHORS

Sam Kaplan currently holds the title of World's Fourth Best Cartwheel Artiste. He is the author of several canonical works of ninja non-fiction, including: *When Ninjas Attack*, *How Hot Is Too Hot?*, *The Art of Brewing The Perfect Tea* and the Tony-nominated off-Broadway play *The Sword and the Chopstick*, now in its third season. He lives in Oakland, California, with his mother.

Keith Riegert is one of the country's leading breeders of seeing-eye tigers for the vision-impaired. A lifelong humanitarian, Keith has spearheaded important international projects such as the Pan-Asian Initiative for the Development of Whiter Rice and the ninja nonprofit Marathon for a Cure for Stab Wounds. He lives in the San Francisco Bay Area with his Malayan tiger, Toast.